# A Practical Guide to Caring for Children and Teenagers with Attachment Difficulties

*of related interest*

**A Short Introduction to Attachment and Attachment Disorder**
*Colby Pearce*
ISBN 978 1 84310 957 0

**Nurturing Attachments**
**Supporting Children who are Fostered or Adopted**
*Kim S. Golding*
ISBN 978 1 84310 614 2

**Understanding Attachment and Attachment Disorders**
**Theory, Evidence and Practice**
*Vivien Prior and Danya Glaser*
ISBN 978 1 84310 245 8

**Big Steps for Little People**
**Parenting Your Adopted Child**
*Celia Foster*
*Forewords by David Howe and Daniel A. Hughes*
ISBN 978 1 84310 620 3

**Fostering a Child's Recovery**
**Family Placement for Traumatized Children**
*Mike Thomas and Terry Philpot*
*Foreword by Mary Walsh*
ISBN 978 1 84310 327 1
**Delivering Recovery Series**

**Understanding Looked After Children**
**An Introduction to Psychology for Foster Care**
*Jeune Guishard-Pine, Suzanne McCall and Lloyd Hamilton*
*Foreword by Andrew Wiener*
ISBN 978 1 84310 370 7

**A Safe Place for Caleb**
**An Interactive Book for Kids, Teens and Adults with Issues of Attachment, Grief, Loss or Early Trauma**
*Kathleen A. Chara and Paul J. Chara, Jr.*
*Illustrated by J.M. Berns*
ISBN 978 1 84310 799 6

**Life Story Books for Adopted Children**
**A Family Friendly Approach**
*Joy Rees*
*Illustrated by Jamie Goldberg*
*Foreword by Alan Burnell*
ISBN 978 1 84310 953 2

# A Practical Guide to Caring for Children and Teenagers with Attachment Difficulties

Chris Taylor

Jessica Kingsley Publishers
London and Philadelphia

First published in 2010
by Jessica Kingsley Publishers
116 Pentonville Road
London N1 9JB, UK
and
400 Market Street, Suite 400
Philadelphia, PA 19106, USA

*www.jkp.com*

Copyright © Chris Taylor 2010

**Library of Congress Cataloging in Publication Data**
Taylor, Chris, 1951-
A practical guide to caring for children and teenagers
with attachment difficulties / Chris Taylor.
p. cm.
Includes bibliographical references and index.
ISBN 978-1-84905-081-4 (alk. paper)
1. Attachment behavior in children. 2. Attachment behavior in
adolescence. 3. Social work with children. I. Title.
BF723.A75T39 2010
362.74--dc22
2009033969

**British Library Cataloguing in Publication Data**
A CIP catalogue record for this book is available from the British Library

ISBN 978 1 84905 081 4

Printed and bound in Great Britain by
MPG Books Limited

*To my mother and father*

# Acknowledgements

This book results from over twenty years' practice in residential care. I would to thank the various staff, too numerous to mention, who I have worked with in safeguarding children, developing therapeutic approaches and promoting recovery.

The material in this book has grown from a series of training courses that I have run and developed over many years. I would like to thank the participants of these courses who have encouraged and inspired me to turn this material into a book, and whose feedback shaped my ideas.

I would like to thank Vivienne Dacre who enabled me to develop training materials, encouraged me to learn and grow, and guided my thinking with wisdom and good humour.

I would also like to thank Maria Taylor, whose therapeutic skill, insight and knowledge inspired my thinking and helped me focus on the essential ingredients of a therapeutic approach.

I would also like to thank several generations of children who I have helped to care for. Their resilience in the face of sometimes immense difficulties and their ability to teach their caregivers underpins everything in this book.

Finally, I would like to thank my family for their support, encouragement and patience.

# Contents

## Chapter Three
## Ways of Caregiving: Working Within the
## Therapeutic Frame

Good enough parenting 68; Hopefulness 68; The engaged self:
why doing is better than talking 69; Mind-mindedness 70; Self-
esteem 71; Parenting styles 73; Planning authoritative care 77;
Discipline 78; Reintegrative shame 82; Sensitive responsiveness
84; Squeezed parenting 86; The transaction with disorganized
attachment 87; Controlling our own arousal 88; The drama
triangle 89; Promoting positive and regulated experiences 94;
Boundaries, consequences and sanctions 95; Power struggles 97

## Chapter Four
## Working for Recovery: Relational
## Representation of the Secure Base

Recovery 100; Promoting a secure base 102; Being 'real' 105;
Trauma and the internal working model 106; Growing up in
therapeutic relationships 107; Re-parenting for recovery 108;
Working with feelings and thoughts 110; Unblocking techniques
112; Empathy 113; Keeping communication open 116;
Unconditional positive regard 116; Saying 'No' 117; Matching
approach to attachment style 118; The anxious child 119

## Chapter Five
## Working with Conflict

The nature of conflict 122; Individual differences in conflict style
122; Inconsistencies in conflict style 124; Choices in conflict
126; Opportunity 128; Attachment patterns and conflict style
128; Keeping yourself safe 129; Communication: 'There are two
people in this' 130; Effective listening 131; Knowing ourselves:
why do adults retaliate? 133; Effective conflict resolution 134;
Assertiveness skills 136; Recovery following conflict 138;
Problem-solving 138

## Chapter Six
## Working with Anger                                     141

Human behaviour 142; Anger in the brain 142; Anger styles 143; Anger: a response to separation 145; Change 146; SAEf charts 146; Anger management training 147; Triggers 148; Low-stress environment 149; The anger cycle 149; Pervasive shame 149; Emotional functioning under stress 150; Managing the situation 150; Whose anger? 151; Trust protection 152; Assertiveness and the angry child 153; Assertive communication 153; Early warning signs 154; De-escalation 154; During the anger storm 158; Plateau 160; Recovery 160; Relationship repair 161; Real anger management: when nobody is angry 162; Relaxation 163; Exercises 165; Anger management worksheets 166

## Chapter Seven
## Managing Challenging Behaviour                         169

Challenging behaviour 170; Challenge or opportunity? 171; Coercion cycle 174; What keeps a problem going 175; Inner world of the child 176; Intervening 177; Aggression 178; Passive-aggressive children 180; Working with violence 182; Deceitfulness 183; Verbal communication 184; Parenting skills 186; Golden nuggets for managing challenging behaviour 189

## Chapter Eight
## Changing Problem Behaviour                             191

Approaches to changing problem behaviour 192; Strategies, techniques and approaches 193; Behaviour modification charts 197

# Introduction

This is a book about a philosophy and model of caring for children and young people with disrupted and painful childhoods that promotes and sustains recovery. It develops a model of therapeutic caring based on extensive practice experience underpinned by a theoretical position that draws on an up-to-date understanding of how attachment influences a child's social, emotional, cognitive and behavioural development.

Workers in this field bring depth of life experience and practice skills to caregiving as part of their daily round. This book turns to attachment theory to provide a focus for these skills and experiences, in order to develop good practice and good care into therapeutic working. By creating and sustaining a safe place in which recovery from early childhood trauma can begin, caregivers promote secure base experiences and develop within the child an organized mental representation of caregiving and affectional bonds.

Whilst it has been written for people working with and living alongside the troubled child: foster carers, residential workers, educators, mental health practitioners, and others, it is also written for those who support them. Workers in these settings are not therapists, but they can be providers of therapeutic experiences, who need to be supported by thoughtful and patient others. Caring for children who have experienced trauma, abuse, violence or neglect is difficult work that requires physical, mental and emotional labour, a deep emotional pool on which to draw, and adequate support from trusted others.

Recovery means change; the child's developmental pathway has unfolded from poor experiences, and a child's therapeutic experience will not take place by accident. It requires a child-centred, planned environment. The planned environment is constructed through education, training and support for caregivers, who are then able to apply useful theoretical perspectives to the work in order to achieve identifiable outcomes. The purpose of this book is to add to the theoretical basis of good consistent care and present practice skills that provide and support a planned environment in which children develop to their full potential. There are no simple answers. However, attachment theory can provide a kind of compass with which to reach hard-to-reach children and young people. The approach presented here is based on six key ideas:

- The child's current experience is most effectively understood with some reference to their early experiences and their mental processes.

- They are the product of all their experiences, not their early experiences alone.

- Developmental difficulties are caused by and sustained by problematic social relationships influencing and being influenced by biological factors.

- The child is actively trying to understand, predict and anticipate their social worlds, which they influence and are influenced by. Although children are therefore potentially autonomous and capable of making choices, these choices are made in a context of earlier developmental experiences and the unfolding developmental pathway.

- Learning occurs within a social context: children learn from adults and from one another.

- The child's ongoing social relationships influence the child's developmental pathway.

## THERAPEUTIC APPROACH AND THERAPY

In writing about these therapeutic approaches to caring for difficult children, little is said about therapy, although there is no intention to dismiss its usefulness. Individual and group therapy can be helpful for some children at some times in their lives. However, a detailed consideration of therapies is beyond the scope of this book, which is concerned with the development of adult caregivers' skills to provide, support and maintain a therapeutic model of care, so that the child's daily experiences are in themselves therapeutic, and provide a secure base from which the child will be able to access therapy when to do so would be helpful. Helpful though therapy can be, there is no magic bullet, no simple way of promoting recovery for the damaged child; repair happens in relationships and relationships happen in daily life. How that daily life is thought about, structured and provided for can be therapeutic. A key skill is for the adults to be able to work with the child's attachment in mind.

## THE CHAPTERS

A practice handbook such as this cannot include everything. There are areas of the work that warrant a book to themselves. Attachment theory provides a framework for thinking about and working with deeply troubled children and young people, many of whom will have multiple difficulties and poor primary experiences. Self-harming behaviour, sexualized behaviour as a reaction to early sexual abuse, and mental health problems cannot be completely covered within the scope of this book.

It is important to acknowledge that although some presenting problems are more readily seen as discrete difficulties, they are sometimes more readily understood to be individualized expressions of disturbing experiences, and many troubled children are not helped by an over-emphasis on presenting problems. What is required is caregivers who are able to remain closely in tune with the individual child's needs, fears and hopes. Sympathy on its own is not enough, and may even be counter-productive. The work also requires empathy: to try to understand from the child's point of view what their world is like. Carl Rogers (1967) emphasized a combination of sympathy and empathy, which he called non-evaluative warmth, as a fundamental quality in any therapeutic relationship. Sometimes looking at the whole person rather than discrete presenting difficulties assists this.

Practitioners are helped to develop creative and effective strategies for helping by having a thorough grasp of attachment development. Chapter 1 lays out the development and current understanding of attachment theory, which underpins subsequent chapters. Chapter 2 advances the concept of a therapeutic environment planned to support recovery from early trauma and unresolved separation and loss. Chapter 3 explores therapeutic ways of caregiving that support this planned environment. Chapter 4 examines approaches towards promoting recovery.

Chapters 5 to 7 focus on practice methods to support the planned environment and build earned security within the child by approaching their presenting difficulties, conflicts, anger and behaviours as therapeutic opportunities. The final chapter considers some traditional behavioural strategies in the light of children and young people with attachment difficulties and early trauma.

## Chapter One

# Patterns of Attachment

Understanding patterns of attachment and the consequences of insecure or disorganized attachment sufficiently to recognize and respond to the attachment needs of young people.

## LEARNING OUTCOMES FOR THIS CHAPTER

Once you have studied this chapter you should be able to:

- outline Bowlby's theory of attachment
- locate attachment relationships
- evaluate factors influencing the development of attachment
- recognize the stages of attachment development
- understand the principle of feedback in attachment security
- recognize the significance of the internal working model (IWM) in human development
- be familiar with categories of attachment
- explain the transactional nature of development and the role of temperament
- understand the significance of attachment organization
- outline the development of controlling behaviours as a response to attachment disorganization
- outline the concept of attachment disorder
- consider the impact of traumatic stress
- contribute to developing a model for recovery by recognizing and responding to a child's attachment needs.

## DEVELOPMENT OF ATTACHMENT THEORY

Since its formulation by John Bowlby (1997), attachment theory has provided important explanations of human behaviour. Developed to explain certain behaviour patterns over the lifespan, attachment theory was always concerned with both normal development and the origin, development, and manifestations of mental or behavioural disorders. How we are attached to our first caregiver seems to influence how we relate to other people, how we feel about ourselves, and deeply affects our psychological well-being.

Attachment is a lifelong issue. Relationship patterns established in the early years of life powerfully influence individuals' views of themselves and their subsequent behaviour, as well as their capacity to be self-reflective. The circumstances that elicit attachment behaviour change over time, the ways in which attachments are expressed also change; but, with some prospect of modification, the way in which attachment is organized survives.

Bowlby argued that the mother–child bond is based on instinct. His thinking was greatly influenced by the theory of evolution and the adaptive nature of animal and human behaviour to the environment put forward by Charles Darwin (see Bowlby 1997), and the work of the ethologist Konrad Lorenz. Lorenz (1966) demonstrated that, during a brief initial period, young birds and mammals learn the characteristics of a moving object and then follow that object around. Since the first moving object encountered by the newborn is usually the mother, this imprinting has obvious survival benefits; the young will follow the mother.

Bowlby developed attachment theory from his observation of infants developing attachment to primary caregivers through a repertoire of genetically based behaviours with protection as their biological function. By concentrating on behaviours that were observable and comparable to other species, Bowlby identified readily apparent features of every child's developing repertoire of behaviours: bond formation, separation protests, stranger anxiety and exploratory activities. He demonstrated that infants are powerfully motivated to seek physical contact with their mothers and not to relinquish that contact once it has been obtained. The purpose of this fundamental behaviour is simple – survival. The mother–child attachment bond is a direct expression of the genetic heritage of our species. Although learning plays an important role in the process, it proceeds on the basis of instinct. Infants bond to their mothers because they are innately programmed to do so from birth.

Attachment has two competing drives: proximity seeking and exploration. Seeking to be near the attachment figure is at the heart of attachment. The child's drive to be secure by keeping close to the attachment figure, who provides a safe haven, and guarantees care, protection and security, competes with the drive to explore and play, where the attachment figure provides a secure base from which to explore the world.

## THE ATTACHMENT RELATIONSHIP

Infant attachment is an internal process that can be classified on the basis of observation of a child's responses at reunion following a period of separation from the attachment figure, and measured as it changes and develops over the lifespan. This pattern of organized behaviour within a relationship with their attachment figure is adaptive to the infant's environment, and equips the child to deal with stressful circumstances and negative emotions, and represents the child's strategy for keeping close to the attachment figure by anticipating their reaction to stress and distress. Attachment is, then, a behavioural system within the child that organizes the child's feelings towards the attachment figure and generates very high levels of positive feelings.

The attachment relationship exists between two people. It is a selective relationship, focused on a particular individual or individuals who elicit attachment behaviour in a manner and to an extent that is not found in interactions with other people. The infant makes an effort to keep close to the attachment figure, relying on this physical proximity for comfort and security. Anxiety and separation distress is expressed when proximity cannot be maintained.

Infants are biologically equipped to form an attachment relationship, and possess attachment responses to bring about the proximity of the caregiver to create safety. Attachment behaviours are the overt means of expressing feelings of danger and safety, switched on in the child by perceived threat and terminated by perceived safety. These are signalling behaviours that communicate with the caregiver to bring their proximity (crying, smiling, and babbling) and approach behaviours (clinging, following, reaching, seeking to be near). At first these behaviours are activated independently, but later they are organized towards the attachment figure, often, but not always, the mother. The attachment bond is seen in the child's distress on separation, relief or joy upon reunion, and how they remain focused on the attachment figure even when they are not in close proximity.

Threats and danger simultaneously activate fear and attachment behaviours in the child. Anxiety is there to keep us safe; fear is the appreciation of danger, and it calls for a response. A range of threats triggers the child's attachment system: threats within the child (when the child is sick, tired, hungry or hurt), threats within the environment (when it is frightening, threatening, or confusing) and threats within the parent or carer (separation, emotional unavailability, inconsistency, rejection).

When care is good enough, activation of the child's attachment behaviours brings increased proximity to the attachment figure, which switches off the attachment behaviours. Conditions that do this vary according to the intensity of the child's arousal. Low levels of distress are soothed by the sight or sound of the attachment figure, especially if the attachment figure acknowledges the child's presence. At a higher intensity of distress, touching or clinging to the attachment figure is needed to switch off the child's attachment behaviours, whereas the highly distressed and anxious child requires symbolic protection from predators, for example, being cuddled for a prolonged time. Separation anxiety occurs when attachment behaviour is activated by the absence of the attachment figure, but cannot be switched off.

Through the predictable provision of such sensitive responsiveness to their distress the child learns to trust and rely on this early relationship. However, these behaviours are only effective if the attachment figure responds. Parenting is to some degree genetically pre-programmed in humans. In evolutionary terms, the great biological cost of reproduction for mothers represents huge parental investment in the offspring and ensures caregivers are oriented to care for every baby by spending time and becoming emotionally bonded, thus ensuring the infant's greatest chance of survival. The strong biological roots of the parental attachment system (referred to as bonding), accounts for the strong emotions that accompany it.

One feature of attachment behaviour is that, irrespective of age, it is accompanied by intense emotions. The kinds of emotions depend on how the attachment relationship is faring. A healthy attachment generates feelings of joy and a sense of security, but when attachment is threatened feelings of jealousy, anger and anxiety arise. When the attachment bond is broken, there are feelings of grief and depression.

## DEVELOPMENT OF ATTACHMENT

From the beginning, infants and parents mutually influence each other. The infant provides cues that convey messages about their state and their needs, for example that they are happy or frightened, hungry, tired or cold etc. It is essential to their welfare that these clues are picked up and appropriately responded to. Also, how the adult behaves exerts an influence on the infant. This is sometimes referred to as contagion. For example, a mother's tensions, which can be picked up through bodily clues and responded to by their baby when they are held, have a marked effect on the nature of interaction.

The choice of attachment figure is not influenced by being the child's biological parents, being female, satisfying physical needs, or providing continuous care. It is the quality of the interaction that is important in order for attachment to develop. Time and/or primary caring do not seem to be in themselves significant. What does matter is that there is fun and playfulness, and sensitive responsiveness to the infant's thoughts and feelings. Individuals who provide fun and playfulness are sought out and are missed when absent. Parents who respond contingently to a child's utterances, by elaborating, developing and negotiating, promote development. Other reinforcing experiences are: feeding, face-to-face play, physical contact, and providing comfort during episodes of distress. The continuous and predictable provision of comfort, shared emotions, shared understanding, safety and the satisfaction of physical needs, in time leads to the development in the infant of trust, security and attachment.

## FOUR STAGES OF ATTACHMENT DEVELOPMENT

Bowlby (1997, pp.265–8) described four stages in the development of attachment, linked to the infant's biological development. Although the boundaries between the stages are not clear-cut, they emerge in a predictable sequence. Bolwby identified the first two months of life as the 'pre-attachment' phase. Infants indiscriminately display signalling behaviours (crying, smiling, babbling) and approach behaviours (clinging, following, reaching), which function to bring about proximity to caregiver.

This stage is followed by 'attachment-in-the-making' (between two and seven months). The developing child has achieved recognition memory and object permanence, and begins to distinguish regular caregivers from other people. Familiar people begin to elicit attachment responses more easily than strangers.

'Clear-cut attachment' develops from seven months to two years. The child's development of recall memory allows them to spontaneously retrieve a representation of the absent person. An enduring relationship is being established: attachment responses are focused on attachment figures and distress on separation is obvious.

From the second or third year onwards a 'goal-corrected partnership' develops. The cognitively developing child is more able to behave intentionally, to plan, and to take into account the feelings and goals of others. If one attachment behaviour does not produce safety or exploration they can substitute another.

## SEPARATION

The developing child's ability to give and receive love depends on the ability of the attachment figure to do so. Security and bonding are crucial to the growth of mature interdependence, which begins in childhood and continues through adolescence and into adulthood. The primal strength of the attachment figure–child bond is vividly illustrated by the loud protests and dreadful despair seen when a young child is forcibly separated from his mother. The extent of suffering and damage caused by separation is broadly related to duration. A brief separation is bad enough; protracted periods of separation can be devastating. Three distinct phases follow enforced separation: protest, detachment and despair.

When this security is threatened, very disturbing emotions are experienced. These memories are stored in an area of the mid-brain known as the limbic system. The limbic system is a collective term referring to several brain parts, including the hippocampus (which processes memory, and is important in emotional regulation) and the amygdala, which is the brain's alarm system and the central generator of flight, flight or freeze responses to threat. These stored memories can later be reactivated by perceived threats to the attachment relationship.. Separation causes most distress from about seven or eight months (attachment-in-the-making) to three years (goal-corrected partnership) by which time the child is able to hold in mind an image of the absent attachment figure.

## ATTACHMENT FEEDBACK SYSTEM

Attachment can be thought of as a feedback system, activated and terminated by situations. The child is testing out whether their wired-in goal (safety/exploration) has been achieved or not, and responds accordingly. A caregiver who is near and attentive encourages sociability in the child, and the child's sociability brings, or keeps, the caregiver near. If separation occurs, the child's attachment behaviours are switched on and bring proximity to the caregiver.

The child is secure in the relationship when they experience both conditions satisfactorily in a way that is 'good enough'. However, when the activated attachment behaviours unpredictably bring about the proximity of attachment figure, or fail to do so at all, the child cannot trust the relationship, and develops anxious and insecure feelings about the attachment relationship.

## SMOTHERING

All children need warmth, love and affection, and safety, but they also need to do things in their own way and to learn from their mistakes. Over-protection and smothering inhibits autonomy. Smothering can show in many ways:

- constantly picking up the child when they are not crying
- not letting the child play as they want, always interfering
- the adult's anxiety over every movement and action
- constant worrying about habits such as eating and sleeping.

The child is over-protected, under-stimulated and 'smothered'. Limited experiences of separation distress do not provide opportunities to realize their own effectiveness by bringing about caregiver proximity through attachment behaviours.

For healthy, secure attachment to develop a child needs to experience both proximity and separation. By bringing proximity to the attachment figure through attachment behaviours, the child learns they are effective in the world and to trust the caregiver.

## INTERNAL WORKING MODEL

An infant's behaviour is not a set of automatic responses, but a vigorous attempt to make sense of what is happening to them. In order to make sense of the world, the developing child forms social concepts of themselves, of the people they interact with, and of the relationships that emerge. From the second year, children begin to represent the world in symbolic form, and construct a symbolic model of themselves, significant others and their relationship with these. This internal working model (IWM) is a mental representation that has emotional and cognitive components. Cognitive components are thoughts, images and beliefs, that is, the things that run through our minds.

The IWM exists outside consciousness and is built on the basis of experience. It is shaped by the outcome of the child's proximity-seeking experiences. The child develops a cognitive representation of the way things are expected to operate, encodes and remembers information consistent with these mental structures, and acts accordingly. Early expectations are transferred onto other people. Once formed, the IWM is imposed like a template on new interactions.

The child's internal representation of the self and their attachment figure develop in a complementary fashion. There are basic differences between the IWM of the child whose proximity-seeking attempts in infancy were accepted, and the IWM of the child whose proximity seeking was blocked or inconsistently accepted. If a child's attachment needs are met, the IWM is of the self as lovable, worthy and effective, and of the other as available, loving, interested and responsive. The child sees themselves as worthy of receiving and able to give love. The relationship represents a secure base from which to explore the world. However, if the child's attachment needs are not met, the IWM of the self is more negative: uninteresting, unvalued, ineffective, unworthy and unwanted, and the IWM represents the other as neglectful, rejecting, unresponsive and hostile. The child cannot find sufficient safety in the relationship, which cannot provide a secure base; reunion is followed not by pleasure but by punishing the absent parent or by rejecting them.

The IWM represents the bridge between the young child's experiences of being cared for and later expectations of others. It influences the child's moods and guides their actions, enabling anticipation of the other person's behaviour, and allowing the child to plan an appropriate response. The IWM becomes a cornerstone of the individual's core beliefs about themselves and others.

With a healthy security the child is able to accept and integrate evidence that questions their core beliefs, but without this security, an individual's view of the self hardens and may become heavily defended. They will unconsciously only accept or even notice information that confirms their core beliefs about themselves, whilst rejecting, disregarding or reinterpreting contradictory information.

After the pre-school period, the IWM tends to be stable over time, although it can be changed by relationship experiences. The attachment relationship has implications beyond the relationship itself as, increasingly, the IWM comes to determine the nature of other social bonds that are formed later.

## ATTACHMENT CLASSIFICATION

Mary Ainsworth (Ainsworth 1985, 1993; Ainsworth and Bell 1970) furthered our understanding of attachment by her pioneering work using the Strange Situation experiment. The Strange Situation is a playroom with a one-way mirror through which observations can be made. The subjects of the experiment are a mother and her one-year-old child who enter the room with an unknown experimenter. After enough time to settle the child and for them to begin playing with the toys the mother leaves the room and the child is left with the stranger. After three minutes, the mother returns, and is reunited with the child. Then both mother and experimenter leave the room and the child is left alone for a further three minutes, after which the mother and child are reunited.

Observations of the child's behaviour patterns at each separation yield a measure of the security of the child's attachment to his mother. Ainsworth identified three contrasting patterns of attachment. The most frequently found reaction to this situation is for children to cry during the separation but then to be easily soothed upon reunion, the children actively sought and maintained proximity to their mothers, and any distress was clearly related to their mothers' absence. The children also preferred their mothers to the stranger. Ainsworth classified this as a secure attachment pattern.

However, some infants shunned contact with their mother on reunion, either ignoring her when she returned to the room or mingling welcome with other responses such as turning away, averting their gaze and moving past her. The stranger and the mother were treated in similar ways. The children were also inhibited in their play. Ainsworth classified this as an insecure attachment of the anxious/avoidant type.

A third pattern of response was typified by infants who were very upset when their mother left the room and were not easily comforted on her return. They resisted contact, but combined this with some proximity seeking. They showed anger towards their mother and gave the impression of being ambivalent about reunion after separation. They also resisted comfort from the stranger. Ainsworth classified this as another insecure attachment of the type anxious/ambivalent (now also referred to as anxious/resistant due to the child's resistance to comfort from the attachment figure following reunion).

Ainsworth backed up her laboratory findings by conducting home observations. Before conducting the Strange Situation experiment, Ainsworth and her team visited the mothers and their infants in their own homes over the babies' first year. They found a high correlation between the experimental results and the quality of the mother–child relationships they had observed. Mothers of the securely attached children were essentially responsive to their babies. Mothers of the anxious/avoidant group were unresponsive; mothers of the anxious/ambivalent group were inconsistently responsive. Each of these types can therefore be understood as an adaptive strategy that the child has adopted in relation to his mother's behaviour.

A further category, anxious-ambivalent, emerged from reassessment by Main and Soloman (1986) of Ainsworth's observation data of difficult-to-classify infants. They found that some children did not show a new pattern of behaviour, but instead lacked a coherent, organized strategy for dealing with separation distress. Anxious-ambivalent represents a breakdown of consistent and organized strategy of emotion regulation, and indicates the child's inability to resolve experiences of stress and anxiety because the attachment figure represents both a safe haven and a source of fear.

The disorganized child's observable attachment behaviours superficially resemble one of the organized categories, and so disorganized attachment is best understood not as a classification itself, but as a dimension that can accompany any other classification. This generates sub-groups: anxious-avoidant, anxious-secure and the most common, anxious-resistant.

Disorganized attachment is always insecure. It is an attempt by the child to create some sort of security for themselves, however distorted or self-defeating this may be. Anxious-secure does not imply a contradiction, but tells us that the child exhibits behaviours that resemble the secure group. In some cases, the disorganization of attachment is so predominant that a secondary, organized strategy cannot be detected.

Ainsworth (1985) was also able to demonstrate that early attachment patterns would impact on the child's future life. Children judged to be securely attached at one year have a longer attention span, are more skilful at handling conflict with their peers, and are more confident and resilient than children who were insecurely attached. This supports Bowlby's view that the child who has become securely attached to a mother or primary caregiver who is responsive to their needs builds up an internal working model of themself as being worthy of receiving and giving love. In contrast, the anxious-avoidant child will form an internal working model of themself as being unworthy of love, needing to conceal their anger and despair at their attachment figure's rejection, or risking driving them away altogether. The anxious-ambivalent child's internal working model is also of an unlovable self, but they conceive the unpredictable primary caregiver as needing to be coerced into granting affection.

Although children who are highly anxiously attached are at increased risk, insecure attachment is not in itself an indicator of later social, emotional difficulties or psychopathology. However, children with disorganized attachment are vulnerable as children and adults to mental ill-health.

## TEMPERAMENT AND ATTACHMENT PATTERN

Temperament is the biologically rooted individual differences in a child's habitual style of responding to people and events. It is highly influential in the development of personality, and can be seen as influencing an individual's behaviour in a wide variety of settings. Personality is a rather vague and ill-defined term. It is generally agreed that personality emerges late on in development, during adolescence or early adulthood, and is a more active organization by the person than temperament. Personality has other components, such as identity, and values and attitudes, overlaying biologically rooted temperamental characteristics. Temperament does not mean that a child shows a particular behaviour. Rather, it explains the coherence of a child's behaviour across settings and time, and identifies underlying regularities within a changing behavioural repertoire and shifting relationships.

Temperament influences three broad areas of behaviour. First, a child's emotional responses: the quality of their mood, reactions to unfamiliar people and settings, and their tolerance to internal states such as hunger and boredom. Second, attention: how readily a child can be comforted, how easily they can be distracted. Third, activity level: the vigour and frequency of activity, and ability to modify activities appropriately.

The child's socio-emotional environment provides a developmental niche in which to grow and develop. In the child's early development, the developmental niche is strongly shaped by the beliefs and values of primary caregivers. When the demands, attitudes and expectations of parents, carers or teachers match the child's temperament, optimal development occurs; there is 'goodness of fit'. Where the characteristics of the individual and environment do not match, distorted development and maladaptive functioning occur.

In a developmental niche that matches the child's needs, a child's difficult temperament does not lead to behavioural difficulties. Disturbing behaviour results from a paucity of fit between the demands and expectations of the social environment and the capacities, motivations and behavioural style of the child.

Children who have a difficult temperament, and grow up in a developmental niche that does not meet their needs (including poverty and social exclusion), are at greater risk of poor outcomes. A difficult temperament is therefore seen as a risk factor for children who are in difficult circumstances. Although an easy temperament is a protective factor, it is no guarantee of an easy life. If there is a mismatch in the developmental niche, parent and child experience stress.

It is simplistic to see the developmental niche shaping the development of a child's behaviour as a one-way process. It is more accurate to think of child and environment as being in a relationship where each influences, and is influenced by, the other. The child plays a significant role in producing their own experiences, both directly by selecting activities, and indirectly by the influence their behaviour has on caregivers. The developmental niche is a changing social environment shaped by the child and the parent, who continue to influence each other as part of a dynamic, transactional process.

Paucity of fit between the environment and the child's temperament is stressful and damages self-esteem; the child feels like a square peg pushed into a round hole. Layered on top of the child's temperamental predisposition is their learning. Behaviour, which expresses their innate predisposition and their learning, shapes their developmental niche. Children who are perceived as difficult pose the greatest challenge to their caregivers, and as temperament is largely inherited, children and parents may share difficult temperaments.

Temperament may therefore be a risk factor for insensitive or harsh caregiving and the development of insecure or disorganized attachment. However, beyond this causal link, there is little to suggest that temperament of itself influences attachment development, and a series of studies on temperament and attachment pattern confirm that environmental factors are decisive in the development of attachment security.

## STRENGTH OF ATTACHMENT

The quality of an attachment is not seen in how the child and caregiver relate, but in how they deal with disruption. The security of the child's attachment is seen in how confident the child is that the attachment figure will be there when they are needed. The strength of attachment differs from the security. It is the intensity with which attachment is displayed, and is not an indicator of security (notice the loyalty of some children who have been abused by parents).

A strong attachment can be a formidable obstacle. Even if parents are not able to provide 'good enough' care, they are still providing much that the child requires: food and shelter, comfort when distressed, teaching of simple skills, continuity of human care, experience that there is someone to whom he is of value. However, without attachment security, the child is investing heavily in a relationship that is not good enough. The security and strength of the attachment are highly influential in the development of the child's internal working model.

## PATTERNS OF ATTACHMENT

Attachment is a pattern of organized behaviour within a relationship, not a trait that children have in varying quantities. Attachment allows the child to feel safe in strange environments and to move away from the attachment figure, physically and emotionally, and explore. Rather than discrete categories, attachment patterns are perhaps more usefully thought of along a dimension. Anxious-avoidant attachment organization results in attachment behaviours being suppressed, whereas anxious-ambivalent (or resistant) attachment organization leads to attachment behaviours being expressed.

A significant majority of children show a secure attachment at age two; others present some insecurity in their attachment, but are not significantly impaired in their functioning. Others, who have experienced more extreme sub-optimal parenting, will have considerable anxiety about their attachment relationship. These children may be increasingly insecure and anxious in their attachment patterns, but are still able to internally organize their response to the attachment figure to have their attachment needs met. However, at the far extreme, other children have experienced the attachment figure as a source of fear, and their attachment is extremely anxiety provoking.

## SECURE ATTACHMENT

Secure attachment is not the same as dependency. Secure attachment is associated with exploration and independence. Granting proximity promotes autonomy rather than inhibiting it. A secure attachment can be described as a long-enduring, emotionally meaningful bond to a particular individual who returns those feelings, in which both adult and child find happiness and satisfaction. The carer is available, sensitive, predictable, and able to repair relationships. The child learns through play, understands their own and other's mental states, and understands and uses emotions. Their thoughts and feelings are integrated. The child has an IWM of the self as lovable, worthy and effective, and a corresponding model of the attachment figure as loving, available and responsive. The relationship is a secure base from which to explore the world. The child who develops a secure attachment can more readily develop:

- resilience

- independence

- compliance

- empathy

- control over their feelings

- social competence

- positive feelings

- healthy self-esteem.

# INSECURE ATTACHMENT

## Unresponsive caregivers: anxious-avoidant attachment

The carer is rejecting, intrusive and controlling. As the child experiences predictable danger (e.g. of being neglected) they change their behaviour to placate others. They are reluctant to experience feelings. Exploration is at the expense of proximity seeking. As an infant, the child may be 'good' (a quiet baby), but there will be failure to thrive. At the extreme, the child will show little sign of negative emotions, and little anxiety at separation, as the child protects themselves from constant, unregulated stress through dissociative defensiveness.

In the face of attachment insecurity, the child develops cognitively organized coping strategies, but is emotionally bereft and hides their emotions from others and from themselves, as if they are all container and no feelings. They may tend to neurotic, internalizing behaviours, and are fearful and anxious. They switch off attachment behaviour, and become overly self-reliant and independent. They may be compulsively compliant, changing their behaviour to please the attachment figure to have their primary needs met. They may inhibit their own negative feelings in order to avoid rejection, and display positive feelings to elicit attention from carers. They are avoidant, defended and may show compulsive traits (experiencing irresistible impulses to act). Later in life they may be over-achieving or show developmental delay. As adults, they may dismiss their own child's attachment needs, and may be overly oriented on success.

The child has an IWM of the self as unlovable and of little worth, and a corresponding model of the attachment figure as unavailable, intrusive and interfering. They trust predictions experienced as thoughts over their feelings.

## Inconsistent caregivers: anxious-ambivalent/resistant

The carer is inconsistently available and insensitive. As an infant they may have been a fretful baby, who has long periods of negative emotions, with strong displays of anger and anxiety. At the extreme, the child fears being ignored and emotionally abandoned, and pursues proximity seeking at the expense of exploration, and may suffer from poor impulse control, be in a state of constant, unregulated stress (hyper-arousal), and show perpetual signs of distress and irritability. It is as if they are all feelings and no container. There is little connection in the child's mind between their behaviour and the carer's response. They may develop poor social competence and low autonomy.

In the face of attachment insecurity, the child develops emotionally organized coping strategies, and is reluctant to think about feelings. They are ambivalent and coercive in their relationships, are easily angry and tend to be obsessive (subject to persistent, intrusive thoughts, ideas or impulses that cause significant unease or anguish). Rather than endlessly adapting to what they think will please the attachment figure, the anxious-ambivalent child will attempt to coerce the attachment figure to meet their primary needs. They tend to show anti-social and externalizing behaviours, and to be non-compliant, and may be deceitful and aggressive. They have mood swings, and excessive tantrums beyond the usual age range, and displays of vulnerability to elicit nurturance. They trust predictions experienced as feelings over thoughts. The child has an IWM of the self as unlovable and ineffective, and the attachment figure as unavailable and unresponsive.

## DISORGANIZED ATTACHMENT

An important difference exists between children who have attachment organization and those who are disorganized. Although a child may be insecure in their attachment to the primary caregiver, anxious-avoidant and anxious-ambivalent adjustments are adaptive responses to their caring environment. The child has an organized, repeatable strategy to have attachment needs met, and an organized mental representation of the attachment figure, and can adjust their behaviour accordingly. However, when the attachment figure is the source of fear (e.g. in cases of infant incest) and/or is not able to provide any predictable care, the child may not be able to develop a mental representation of the attachment figure, or an organized, repeatable strategy to gain safety. As well as being insecurely attached, such children are also disorganized in their pattern of attachment. They are at significant risk of developing later difficulties.

### No strategy/multiple strategies: disorganized attachment

The carer has no strategy for parenting, or unpredictably employs multiple strategies, often as a consequence of drug use, psychiatric illness, domestic violence and abuse and neglect.

The child has little ability to cope; they make unpredictable use of coping strategies seen in anxious-avoidant and anxious-ambivalent children. The attachment figure, the source of safety, is also the source of fear. As the child cannot predict danger they are in a state of constant vigilance. Left in a state of fear without solution, they are fearful and helpless, and live in a state of high arousal and unregulated emotions. They express fear, anger and violence, and are dazed, confused, and apprehensive. The child has no coherent system for dealing with separation, and is likely to experience an intrusive need for comfort, with a significant risk of promiscuity with strangers. Fear is intrusive, and they experience sudden inhibition of emotions. They have little response to pain, and unpredictable intrusion of anger.

As an adult, they are likely to remain disorganized and disturbed, and be unable to meet the needs of their own children. The child has an IWM of the self as powerful yet bad, and the attachment figure as frightening and unavailable. Without attachment organization, the child is left with the insoluble problem of fear and safety being represented by the attachment figure. They are caught in a relationship that continually presents them with an approach–avoidance dilemma, not knowing which choice provides safety: to get proximity to the attachment figure or to avoid them.

By age six, although some children remain insecure-disorganized and behaviourally disorganized, with no coherent strategy for proximity seeking, children with disorganized attachment may have developed a form of behavioural organization that represents a kind of role reversal. The child acquires control in the relationship with the attachment figure, who initiates this role reversal by showing helplessness in the face of the child's distress.

These children have developed a compulsive need to control those around them in an attempt to resolve the paradox of frightened or frightening attachment figure, and regulate their emotions and behaviours by controlling the source of unintegrated fears. In compensation for the chaos of their inner world, they develop a fragile overlay of coping behaviours that are either controlling and punitive, or controlling and caregiving. Despite the apparent organization of the controlling child's behaviour, their underlying, internal representations are by no means organized.

Punitive-controlling behaviours seek to keep the attachment figure from occupying the role of the carer, as it is too frightening to let the helpless/hostile carer be in control. The child begins to be hostile, aggressive and directive towards the attachment figure. Interactions are intended to humiliate them into submission, or aggressively control the attachment figure. The child takes responsibility for their own care and protection and never seeks adult advice, guidance or protection. They generalize these controlling behaviours onto other adults.

Overbright-caregiving behaviours develop when the attachment figure's needs, vulnerabilities and dependencies take precedence over the child's. The child is frightened by the adult's helplessness and cannot find an attachment strategy to increase security. As a way of attempting to engage the attachment figure, the child begins to act like a parent towards the adult, who responds by emphasizing their own dependence on the child's precocious qualities. The child directs the parent's interaction in a helpful, positive manner, and is excessively cheery, polite and helpful. They are orientated to protect the parent. The child's needs are suppressed and remain beneath the child's petrified surface, erupting as rage or panic when the child is under pressure.

## ATTACHMENT DISORDER

There continues to be some lack of clarity about the nature of attachment disorder, but it is generally agreed that attachment disorders arise following very adverse early caregiving experiences. Attachment disorder is a diagnosis derived from a cluster of mainly social behaviours that suggests that there is such imbalance in the use of the attachment figure that there is little consistency in preferred attachment figure, whereas disorganized attachment reflects the attachment figure as a source of fear, not safety, leaving the infant unable to deactivate the attachment and restore a sense of security. It may be that attachment disorder is a severe form of disorganized attachment. Attachment disorder diagnosis does not examine the nature of attachment within a dyadic relationship, but generalizes from other social interactions.

Two international classifications are used from DSM-IV (*Diagnostic and Statistical Manual of Mental Disorders, IV, Type Revised*) or ICD-10 (*International Statistical Classification of Diseases and Related Health Problems Tenth Revision*). The DSM-IV TR is used in diagnosing mental disorders in the United States, and is published by the American Psychiatric Association. It uses medical concepts and terms, and states that there are categorical disorders that can be diagnosed by set lists of criteria. This is controversial, and some mental health professionals, and others, question the usefulness of this approach. Because it is produced for mental health specialists, its use by people without clinical training can lead to inappropriate application of its contents. The DSM publishers generally advise that lay people should only consult the DSM to obtain information, not to make diagnoses, and that people who may have a mental disorder should be referred for psychiatric counselling or treatment.

Reactive attachment disorder (RAD) is a clinically recognized form of severe insecure attachment characterized by the breakdown of the child's social ability and markedly disturbed and developmentally inappropriate social relatedness that begins before age five. The DSM classifies children with RAD as so neurologically disrupted that they cannot attach to a primary caregiver, establish positive relationships with other people, or develop normally.

RAD takes two forms: inhibited and disinhibited. In the inhibited form the child shows a persistent failure to initiate or respond to most social interactions, and social responses are inhibited, hyper-vigilant, highly ambivalent and contradictory. They mistrust nearly everyone. In the disinhibited form the child shows indiscriminate sociability and a lack of selective attachment. As they grow older they show indiscriminate social extroversion, treating all people as if they were their best friend.

Confusingly, ICD-10 describes two distinct attachment disorders: reactive attachment disorder of childhood (RAD) and disinhibited attachment disorder (DAD). ICD-10 RAD presents as strongly contradictory or ambivalent responses at separation and reunion, emotional disturbance, with apparent misery, unresponsiveness or withdrawal and aggressive responses to the child's own and to other's distress. Social play is impeded by the child's emotional responses. DAD is described as generally clinging behaviour and/or indiscriminately friendly behaviour associated with emotional and/or behavioural disturbance.

## ADULT ATTACHMENT STYLES

Attachment patterns established in early development are often stable over time; the nature of childhood attachment can strongly influence adult relationships, and can be transferred to the next generation.

The standard, widely used instrument to assess adult attachment is George, Kaplan and Main's Adult Attachment Interview (AAI) (1984, revised 1985, 1996). It takes the form of a semi-structured interview, which is usually recorded. Adults are asked to recall memories from childhood and evaluate them from their current perspective. The semi-structured interview is then transcribed verbatim for coding. Coding is based not on the content of autobiographical memories, but on the way experiences and their effects are reported. Adult attachment styles are categorized under the following headings.

## Autonomous-secure

The autonomous-secure individuals can recall their own earlier attachment-related experiences in an objective and open way, even if these were not favourable. Although this classification is not dependent on a secure attachment as a child, the adult is able to reflect on and discuss attachment experiences openly. They value relationships, and tend to have children who are securely attached.

## Dismissing-detached

Individuals tend to give a very supportive account of parents, unsupported or contradicted by recall evidence. They may not be able to remember attachment-related experiences, and dismiss attachment relationships as of little concern. They tend to have children who are anxious-avoidant.

## Preoccupied-entangled

Individuals are preoccupied with dependency on their own parents, and are still actively trying to please them. Preoccupied-entangled individuals give inconsistent, incoherent accounts of their childhood, and unresolved childhood conflicts remain an issue. They show confused, angry or passive preoccupation with attachment figures. They tend to be parents of anxious-ambivalent children.

## Unresolved-disorganized

The individual had experience of traumatic separation from the attachment figure, and has not worked through the mourning process; or they experienced severe abuse and neglect. They show substantial loss of monitoring and reasoning when recalling attachment-related events. They tend to be parents to children who are disorganized in their attachment. Interviews that are assigned to the unresolved-disorganized pattern are also assigned to the best fitting of the three alternatives.

## Cannot classify

This is a more recent category added in 1996 by Hesse. The individual's discourse shows a combination of contradictory patterns.

# CONTINUITY OF ATTACHMENT PATTERN

During the early years, a child's attachment pattern is a property within a relationship, but for older children it becomes increasingly a property of the child, and is imposed on new relationships. Once a pattern of attachment has developed, it tends to persist over time. Weinfield and colleagues (2004) conducted a long-term study that involved administering the Adult Attachment Interview to a sub-sample from the Minnesota Child Study; this showed a great deal of continuity between infant attachment behaviours and mental representations of attachment at age 19.

Continuing environments support attachment pattern stability. Attachment classifications tend to remain stable over a child's development if they are reinforced by the caregiving environment, but change if adaptation to a new caregiving environment requires it. This confirms the idea that attachment is not a static personal trait, but an adaptive, relational quality. Continuity is particularly strong for disorganized attachment.

# CHILDREN UNDER STRESS

## Stress and stressors

Stress is the reaction people have to exposure to stressors, which can simply be defined as something that threatens our safety or well-being. It arises out of worrying about being able to cope, and results in a physiological imbalance in the body that has unpleasant emotional and cognitive components. Stress is cumulative; an individual may cope with one stressful event in some circumstances, but be unable to cope satisfactorily with similar events when facing additional stressful circumstances. Some people feel stress in the absence of stressors, and some people do not feel stressed even when faced with a stressor. How we individually manage stress is influenced by the way we interpret or perceive the situation. Interpret things in one way, and we feel stressed, interpret them differently and we feel fine. How many stressors an individual faces also influences how they interpret events. When we feel stressed, we may interpret events as threatening. Atkinson and colleagues (1999) suggest that stressors can be grouped into five types:

- Traumatic events: situations of extreme danger outside usual human experience.

- Uncontrollable events: the less control we have (or perceive we have) the more stress we experience.

- Unpredictable events: being able to predict a stressful event usually reduces its severity.

- Challenges to our limits: events that challenge our capabilities are stressful.

- Internal conflicts: when our inner needs, motivations or beliefs are in conflict with each other.

Children are subject to the usual range of life stress, but these stressors are compounded by a life cut adrift from the past, separated from families, with uncertain futures, and lacking satisfactory regulation of emotions. Negative beliefs about the self and the attachment figure (self–other beliefs) are inherent in the IWM implicit in insecure attachment. These poor self–other beliefs predispose some children to interpret non-threatening events as stressors. The trauma and stress of abuse is often each of these events occurring in the same abusive acts. As the child is unable to protect themselves from, or recover from, this overwhelming stress, events that we might not expect to be perceived as a threat may trigger stress responses in the child in ways that are hard for us to fathom. Under stress, they may revert to the solitary defences that they have used to survive before.

Stress is toxic to the brain and may be addictive: the traumatized child may become used to the high that flows from substantial and frequent doses of stress hormones.

## Traumatic stressors

Trauma is a threat to integrity of oneself or others. In infancy, trauma is more closely related to caregiver's emotions and availability than to events outside the child. When an individual is confronted with traumatic stressors, the attachment system is activated, and triggers seeking for help, comfort and safety. If this safety is not available, or is inconstantly available, the child internalizes these threats as insecurity, and forms a mental representation of themselves as unworthy of protection. If this safety is only available in the source of fear, the child cannot organize their mental representation of safety in the attachment relationship. These insecure internal working models evaluate later attempts at soothing stress as either illegitimate (the child believes that they do not deserve comfort), or as likely to produce a painful interaction with a frightening attachment figure.

With a secure attachment, trauma evaporates easily, but if there is insufficient emotional support, the child's reaction to trauma is denial, and the full weight of their resources is used to protect them as best they can. Panic and insecurity re-activate powerful patterns of feelings first developed in infancy or childhood. The child keeps an area of unreality in his mind, as an escape for when life gets too painful, often resulting in a desire for revenge against childhood injustice, and contradictory feelings of hostility and dependence.

## HOPE FOR RECOVERY

The ability to give a coherent narrative of past relationships is an index of secure attachment. People with a history of insecure attachment experience far greater difficulty in narrating their past. This suggests that an important task of therapeutic working is to help piece together a coherent account of the child's emotional history. In collaboratively working out the details of a child's history a narrative begins to emerge.

The longer recovery is left, the more needs to be recovered from. In a healthy development, a secure attachment develops because the 'good enough' parent fills the child with enough of the 'good stuff'. However, despite the best of intentions of well-meaning carers, the insecurely attached child defends themselves against this 'good stuff', either with cognitively based coping mechanisms or emotional ones, or both.

Recovery comes through relationships and through changes in life circumstances. Although childhood attachment styles tend to be stable into adolescence and adulthood, there is hope for recovery through careful planning of a therapeutic environment, and the skill of engaged carers. Professionals provide the relationships and changed circumstances necessary for recovery by recognizing that attachment behaviours are triggered by perceived threats and terminated by perceived safety. We should recognize and respond to attachment behaviours as a need to feel safe, expressed as seeking to be near, and distress on separation, in an attachment-focused developmental niche: the planned environment.

Children change throughout childhood, and although the ability of areas of the brain to expand their functions diminishes with age, young children can recover through parenting that meets their primary needs. Different relationships and changes in life circumstances can promote cognitive re-evaluation. Although this cognitive re-evaluation is unlikely before adolescence, distortions that exist on the edge of consciousness may be re-evaluated during this period.

## Chapter Two

# The Planned Environment

## An Organizational Representation
## of a Secure Base

Attachment theory is a theory of developmental pathways. Sub-optimal parenting and the child's innate qualities influence each other in a transactional process that determines the child's early developmental pathway. A planned, therapeutic approach supports recovery by providing new emotional and cognitive representations of caregiving that allow the developmental pathway to adjust to responsive parenting. This is the therapeutic environment that supports individual therapy.

## LEARNING OUTCOMES FOR THIS CHAPTER

Once you have studied this chapter you should be able to:

- act as a hopeful role model to promote change
- account for the transactional nature of care
- reflect on hidden beliefs and assumptions
- sustain a planned, therapeutic, environment
- promote positive and regulated experiences within a planned environment
- provide a therapeutic physical environment
- adjust caregiving to placement phase
- understand and contribute to the required organizational structures
- assess and manage therapeutic risk
- evaluate the significance of transitions and plan accordingly
- support a child through daily transitions.

# WHERE CHANGE BEGINS

Secure attachment is a key protective factor against the traumatizing effect of experiences of abuse. Without this protective factor, children who have suffered abuse are more vulnerable to a range of future psychological and emotional difficulties. In 1999, van Ijzendoorn, Schuengel and Bakers-Kranenberg looked at nearly 80 studies conducted over ten years. In western countries they found the largest group of children (approximately 60%) to be securely attached. Resistant and disorganized categories account for about 15 per cent each, and avoidant children are least common (about 7%). However, the disorganized category rises to somewhere between 25 and 35 per cent of children in low-income families. Resistant attachment is more frequent in non-western countries, and disorganized attachment is at about the same level. Children with disorganized attachment are over-represented in groups of children with a range of mental health and behavioural difficulties. Many adults within clinical populations show adult disorganized attachment.

Children with disorganized attachment may also be over-represented in the population in public care. Many children are from low-income families (a risk factor for disorganized attachment). Bringing children into care is a frequent response to extremes of sub-optimal parenting and behavioural difficulties associated with disorganized attachment may be sufficient to trigger care intervention. Growing up in care can be intergenerational: disjointed personal histories may be exacerbated by parents' similar disorganizing experiences.

Institutional care can also disorganize a child's attachment. Frequent changes of placement, discontinuity of caregivers, and inconsistencies in caregiving all replicate the family environments that trigger attachment disorganization. Substitute carers are also unlikely to be able to offer the unconditional love that children need. Even if they were able to do so, external pressures within the care system and wider society will frequently disrupt even successful (for the child) placements. Children are moved from placements in foster families and residential homes for all kinds of reasons. Although some placement moves are clearly in the child's best interest, many are not, and many frontline carers have experienced children being moved for what seems to them and to the child capricious reasons: because they have made progress, and are deemed to be 'no longer so difficult' or 'cured'; because they are so difficult to care for that some other solution is looked for (with a fair amount of searching for magic bullets); for reasons of finance and targets; because individuals with powers over placement decisions decide to. In ways too numerous to mention, the care system itself adds further layers of separation and unresolved loss to the chaotic and traumatized experiences of the children cared for.

This is the system we live with and it is beyond the scope of this book to change, or even address, systemic failings in the care and education of vulnerable children. However, within this shaky, creaky system, committed, insightful, skilled and knowledgeable adults can and do make a difference.

## PLANNING FOR RECOVERY

The traumatized and abandoned child is not some free-floating individual with less than good enough coping mechanisms. They are living and surviving as best they can in a social environment that contains both constraining and enabling factors. Poor attachment experiences affect brain development, notably the pre-frontal cortex, the area of the brain associated with how our thoughts are able to control our feelings, and as a consequence, children with attachment difficulties may have poor impulse control. Early traumatic memories may leave them in a state of constant, unregulated stress (hyper-arousal), constantly scanning for threats (hyper-vigilance), which further damages relationships.

Humans are evidence-seeking creatures. We understand social relationships by processing the information we receive in our social exchanges and environment: evidence that things are one way or another. And our point of view is coloured by our experiences, including our relationship history. Many of the children we work with will have internalized a view of relationships as not 'good enough', their internal working model, which exists at the edge of consciousness, distorts the child's perception of relationships. Anxiously attached children need only a little evidence to support their IWM, which becomes stronger and more deeply embedded in a kind of self-fulfilling prophecy. However, they require consistent, prolonged and stable experience of human relationships that contradict the IWM to provide evidence to challenge hidden and distorted self-beliefs.

The evidence of experience that not all interactions are as predicted by the IWM challenge it, and over time the child can begin to think differently about human relationships. Where does this evidence that challenges these constructs come from? From the relationships the child has with their caregivers. Therapeutic relationships are unlikely to develop by chance. Relationships are transactions, and even well-meaning and skilled adults can be blown off course by the child's anxiety and hostility.

Caregivers can provide group living within a consistent, predictable, nurturing and stimulating environment that goes some way to help children to a more balanced way of dealing with the world, and to begin to use information from both emotions and cognition in a flexible way. This is an emotionally holding environment that gives the child the experience that their difficult, disturbing and uncontainable emotions can in fact be held and contained, and so represents the important and often missing primary experience that leads to developing a sense of trust and the ability to think and feel.

This is the general therapeutic milieu that enables the growing sense of self-worth that is necessary for participation in therapy. Therapeutic living deals with emotion, but does not demand an emotional commitment from the child to the adults. Rather, it seeks to help the child develop emotional literacy through the provision of warmth, high expectation and high explanation. Predictable care from skilled and knowledgeable adults will, over time, help the child better manage their anxiety arousal, and experience that interactions with others can be predictable.

Over time, consistent availability, a pervading sense of unconditional positive regard, and a nurturing response to need counter-balance the primary experience of unavailable adults, and promotes the healthy development of self-esteem and self-worth. A structured socio-emotional environment allows for the experience of positive social interactions, the introduction of positive feelings into play, and an increasing cognitive appreciation of consequences and responsibility for actions. With the uncertainty of placements in mind, it is important to hold onto some key thoughts. Even in settled placements, adults move on for all kinds of reasons (many of them good) and they cannot, nor should they, put aside completely their own needs (or those of their families) for the attachment needs of the Looked After child. Within foster care, deeply committed adults can hold out the prospect of the anxiously attached child experiencing something close to the maternal preoccupation of one person that is missing from their primary experiences; however, it can be difficult to replicate this in group-care settings, where many of the most troubled children are cared for, and even the most dedicated and committed workers may be separated from the child through one or other moving on long before recovery has progressed sufficiently to support the child to cope with another loss.

In group care, a more satisfactory approach is that, rather than focusing on the relationship between the child and one key carer, the parenting group, acting within the developmental niche, provide the preoccupation that the child requires: the experience of being held in mind. Providing unconditional positive regard and authentic warmth, the group of adults and the placement setting become a symbolic attachment figure, representing a safe haven at times of threat and providing a secure base from which to explore current relationships.

In order for foster carers or the parenting group to become a symbolic attachment figure for the child, the organizational structures around caring for the child should reflect the same ethos and core values as the model of care. Caregivers will need this level of support if they are to survive this difficult task. Interactions between adults, and between groups and other professionals, should mirror the healthy human relations model that underpins the child's care. Separations that arise from the mechanisms of the care system should be well planned for and explicitly dealt with.

Whether the setting is a children's home, foster care, education or some other place where the inner world of the child is thought about and their primary needs are answered, the planned environment stands symbolically and practically for the role and function of the attachment figure: to provide the trusting, reliable and sensitive interactions that engender secure attachment.

## A TRANSACTIONAL PROCESS

Children are looked after by others in order that the care they receive can influence their development in a positive way. This is often seen as a straightforward process of adults guiding children towards desired outcomes. However, this ignores the way children are actively involved in constructing their development in what is a two-way or transactional process, environment and child influencing each other. The child is not a passive recipient of developmental experiences; they actively construct their own environment, their place in the group, and their one-to-one relationships as they explore their unique developmental pathway.

In a child-centred model of care, the child's needs remain at the centre of these transactional interactions; their developmental niche is sensitively responsive to their needs. However, the terrifying primary experiences of loss and abandonment that pervade the child's inner world exert a powerful pressure on this developmental niche, which can easily begin to mirror the child's early experiences. Skilful, caring adults can lose focus on their professional skills and respond intuitively to the child in ways that reinforce the child's core beliefs about themselves, significant others, and the nature of relationships.

Key to sustaining this planned environment is understanding the child's inner world. We may recognize elements of their inner world from our experience as practitioners, but each individual's thoughts and feelings must also be explored with them. However difficult it is for the child to cope with their lives, they are experts in their experiences. Communication is crucially important. Not only must we be skilled at communicating with the child, but we must also be skilled and patient at unravelling their communication with us.

For any of us, it is difficult to communicate our inner world; we mostly do so through symbolism and metaphor. Inevitably, for the children who we look after, the bleak terror of their primary experiences is disturbing, for them and for us. Their communication, which is unlikely to be rational or civilized, requires us to recognize and contain it, and to assist them in interpreting it. This can only happen safely within trusting relationships. It is the worker who is emotionally close to the child who is well placed to do this. The continuous and predictable provision of comfort, shared emotions, safety and satisfaction of physical needs in time leads to a sense of trust, earned security and attachment.

For this process of change to begin, relationships require the support provided by a planned environment. The planned environment exists in the wider cultural background and social environment, and is constructed from four domains:

- caregiver beliefs and values
- the physical environment
- the organizational ethos
- caregiving practices.

## BELIEFS AND ASSUMPTIONS

The developmental niche in which a child's life unfolds is greatly influenced by the beliefs and values held by caregivers. We all have core beliefs about childcare, and these core beliefs generate underlying assumptions that trigger automatic thoughts about how to react to the child's world. The degree to which our beliefs and assumptions match the child's needs influences how far the socio-emotional environment can contribute to the child's recovery. A mismatch between the child's needs and the developmental niche is stressful for all concerned. In order to work therapeutically with the child, caregivers need to be prepared to examine these core beliefs and reflect on their usefulness or otherwise in promoting the child's recovery.

Although this is a challenging task, it is also a rewarding one, as we grow individually by looking at ourselves in this way. It can help to remember that this is no more than we are asking the child to do: to look at their beliefs, values, attitudes and behaviours and change unhelpful aspects of their lives. Daniel Hughes (1997) suggests some basic assumptions that it is helpful to make about the child.

- The child is doing the best they can.

- They want to improve.

- Life now is a living hell.

- In order to stay safe, they will try to control everything.

- They will avoid anything painful or stressful.

- Their attacks on you reflect a lack of trust of your motives, poor emotional control, fragmented thinking, pervasive shame, and a lack of impulse control.

- To change these children will need us to accept, comfort and teach them, validate their sense of self whilst teaching important developmental skills, and fine tune our expectations to their developmental age so that they can experience success, not failure.

- Under stress, they may revert to solitary defences that they have used to survive before.

- They will have to work hard to learn how to live well.

- We cannot do the work for them, nor can we save them.

- We can comfort, teach, respect and value them.

- We will need support and guidance from trusted others.

- We will make mistakes; it is important to face them and learn from them, which is what we ask the child to do.

Beliefs and assumptions such as these unconditionally value the child whilst protecting us from being overwhelmed by their inner world. This is the basis of the therapeutic alliance that is the child's best additional resource.

## THE HOLDING ENVIRONMENT

Infants experience being held physically when they are picked up and cuddled, and emotionally when the caregiver is able to contain the child's most unthinkable and primitive thoughts. This holding of frightening feelings allows the child to develop the ability to make sense of their experiences and develop the ability to think and feel. When this relationship is missing, the child may be left with either a chaotic inner world, or very little awareness of the differences between their own inner world and other people's experiences and feelings. People may see such a child as wildly unpredictable, out of touch, manipulative and violent, which is how the world around them appears to the child, without the capacity to trust themselves or anyone else. The child is likely to feel incurably different, suspicious and defensive, able to somehow attach themselves to some adults and completely reject others, trying to play adults off against each other as good and bad. They are likely to be afraid of their own violence, and the fear of the adults merges with this fear, making them more panicky and more violent.

Adults looking after these children have to supply functional control themselves, and hold both the child and the violence together. Confrontation is not helpful. What is required is calmness, quiet, and a sufficient number of adults to hold on to and contain the violent emotions. At times this can seem like an impossible task. Adults can feel impoverished and exhausted by the scale of the demands placed on them.

The totality of the caregivers' physical and metaphorical holding can be thought of as a holding environment. The holding environment consists of a number of key elements:

- Primary needs for security, warmth, containment and stimulation are met unconditionally.

- There are appropriate and explicit boundaries on behaviour and the expression of emotions; strong feelings can be expressed but do not get out of hand.

- There is a commitment to resolving misunderstandings.

- There is giving and tolerance in relationships, so that individuals feel genuinely cared for and looked after.

- There is some degree of interpretation or reaching out in communication.

- The child is thought about. Even when the adult is not close by the child is held in mind.

We need to be able to show the child that we can feel their anxious feelings without collapsing. By appropriately containing our own anxiety, we show the child that we are not overwhelmed by their powerful and uncontained emotions. As the adult and child manage these feelings together, until the child is able to do so alone, the child gains a direct experience that these powerful feelings are not overwhelmingly destructive, and over time has the opportunity to internalize this experience to begin to contain their own feelings.

Appropriate holding for the caregivers who are engaged in the holding process is essential. The quality of the holding environment for carers determines the quality of the holding environment for the child. People under stress may interpret things in a distorted way. When working with very troubled children adults can feel unsafe, and un-held, leading to feelings of being under-valued or persecuted. By working towards maximum clarity in communication, and showing commitment to resolving misunderstandings, these feelings can be acknowledged and contained.

In order to develop mentally the child must experience that they are not forgotten. Care and thinking need to be underpinned by attentiveness to the child that represents the primary maternal preoccupation of a mother with a newborn infant. This relies on the culture in which thinking is embedded: how physical and structural holding are founded on adults thinking together about the child.

## THE PLANNED ENVIRONMENT

Attachment is there to keep us safe. Without the safety of secure attachment, the ability to regulate emotions develops less readily. Insecurely attached children may be functioning at a level of persistent unregulated emotions, or hyper-arousal, which may be compounded by trauma, the further imprinting of fear. The holding environment is a planned socio-emotional environment. It is a low-arousal, low-stress environment in which adults set and maintain the emotional tone.

The low-arousal environment is woven from consistent, predictable, nurturing, and stimulating care, with explicit boundaries that meet the needs of the child. This engenders a growing sense of trust, security and attachment. Within an overall environment that is child centred, adults set and maintain an emotional tone suitable for the developmental level of the child and conducive to recovery. They must establish themselves as trustworthy, and be truthful and compassionate, working with openness, collaboration and consent.

At the heart of attachment security is the notion of a secure emotional base, which supports exploration by watching over the child, delighting in them, and helping when necessary, and welcoming their return, protecting, comforting, delighting in the reunion, and organizing their feelings. The child or adolescent can explore the world around them, and return, knowing that they will be welcomed, physically and emotionally nourished, comforted, and reassured. The provision of a secure base requires that the parental figure is available and ready to respond: to encourage and assist, but to intervene only when necessary. Caregivers work to provide a circle of security through interacting aspects of parenting:

- sensitive responsiveness, shown in the use and expression of empathy and the naming and containing of feelings
- availability, shown in responding to the child's true needs, not their over- or under-dependence
- acceptance of the child for who they are, shown in unconditional positive regard, and supported through developing healthy self-esteem so that the child is both valued and able to value themselves
- collaboration that promotes autonomy and models co-operation
- belonging in a warm, comfortable, accepting and supportive environment.

In order to provide this secure base, parental figures require a developed understanding of the individual child's attachment behaviour as an intrinsic aspect of human nature, and they need to understand that the expression of attachment behaviours later in life is neither regrettable nor regressive, as it is often labelled, but a result of the individual attempting to find a secure base with an available attachment figure. Secure base experiences are threatened by unpredictable and inconsistent caring, and traumatized children's emotional arousal can undermine the predictability of the environment. Group-care teams need to find satisfactory methods to provide consistent and predictable care in order to provide secure base experiences.

A child's level of emotional arousal goes up and down according to their response to stimuli. We should know how to influence this arousal in order to be able to provide a planned emotional environment for the child.

Although initially the carers assume responsibility for regulating the child's arousal, the goal is that eventually the child will be able to regulate their own emotions in an age-appropriate way. Therefore the therapeutic environment provides a balance between lowering arousal and stimulation.

## A SECURE BASE – LEVERS OF AROUSAL

This balance is brought about through the caregiver understanding levers that affect the child's emotional tone, and influencing those levers in sensitive responsiveness to the child's needs. The therapeutic caregiver is sensitively responsive to the child's need for each of these behaviours and engages in all four with fun and playfulness. As the provision of this balance is led by the need of the child, it is in itself nurturing. As it is thought about individually, it avoids institutionalization and oppression, and holds the child safely in an emotionally contained environment in which the adults set and maintain the emotional tone. The levers of arousal are Structure, Nurture, Soothing Nurture and Challenge. Structure, nurture and soothing nurture represent a safe haven. They manage emotional arousal and stress downwards; under perceived or imagined threat, the child can return to this safe haven for protection and proximity. Challenge promotes exploration from a secure base.

Structure reduces arousal levels, and is provided by being consistent with expectations and explanations, and predictable in our attitudes and responses. The child is likely to have experienced highly unpredictable caregiving, a major contributor to attachment insecurity and disorganization. A predictable attitude engenders a sense of safety in the relationship and over time allows the child to feel secure in their relationship with the caregiver. Predictability should also include predictable routines, which reduce feelings of uncertainty and threat, and predictable responses to the child's actions, both wanted and unwanted.

Structure also requires explicit boundaries, and high levels of explanation. Activities and events have definite beginnings and endings, and the child learns it can be fun to follow the adult's lead. Through structure, the child learns about order in their environment, and as well as being reassured that the adult is in control, because expectations are explicit, the child has a secure enough base to learn self-control. Structure requires carers to give directions that are clear and specific.

A simple and effective way of providing sufficient structure is to agree an explicit and regular structure to the day. All children require a degree of routine, but the anxiously attached children often do not cope well with unpredictability and change. It is not enough that they should be able to enjoy variety or accept change because of their chronological age; they are likely to panic and to revert to primitive coping methods to maintain a sense of control. An explicit structure to the day provides a basic sense of safety and predictability; it also promotes understanding of what is expected of the child. Routines are better expressed in terms of what the child is to do, rather than what they are not allowed to do.

Clear daily structures should also evolve with the child, and should be planned taking account of the child's developmental age as well as their chronological age. For example, an older child's bedtime may need to be age appropriate, but their settling routine of soothing nurture may need to meet their developmental age. Nurture, the warm, unconditional and predictable provision of basic needs, maintains the child at their level of arousal. It emphasizes to the child the importance of the adult in a caregiving role: soothing, calming, quieting, caretaking activities that make the world safe, predictable, warm and secure. This reassures the child that adults provide comfort and stability and meets the child's unfulfilled younger needs, and helps the child to be able to relax and allow themselves to be taken care of. Nurture builds the inner representation that the child is lovable and valued, and focuses on the child's uniqueness. Physical touch is used in a safe and positive way. All nurturing activities should allow the child to feel comfortable at their developmental age.

Challenge and stimulation promote exploration and help the child take age-appropriate risks. They promote feelings of competence, confidence and autonomy, and include high expectations of the child, and wider experiences such as education and social interactions. In order to build confidence, it is often necessary to begin challenge below the child's emotional age, slowly increasing expectations. Over time, the child learns to feel a sense of pride in their accomplishments and learns that others are also pleased with their progress.

Although insecurely attached children require high levels of predictability, life cannot, nor should it be, completely predictable. There is an inevitable tension between consistency and flexibility. As well as experiencing predictability and consistency, all children need to experience a degree of uncertainty and variation. A planned routine that is always followed can lead to a feeling of institutionalization, the routine becoming more important than the child. A degree of flexibility and change provides constructive challenge to the child's coping and needs to be woven into a structured routine in a careful way. However, changes should be for good reasons that can be made explicit and explained to the child. Within the change, the child's needs must still be met, and the agreed routine should be re-established when circumstances allow.

Soothing nurture is a kind of emotional first aid kit that provides a powerful representation of the protective proximity of the attachment figure. It includes activities that can be used to soothe a distressed or over-aroused child. Arousal can be reduced by providing emotional warmth and soothing experiences (e.g. brushing hair, cuddles, rhythmic rocking, a protecting light at bedtime, a bedtime story, etc.). Children who are soothed when aroused learn to self-soothe; the child who needs us to read a bedtime story to soothe and settle them may eventually learn to soothe themselves by reading before bed. Soothing can be experienced through any of the senses, and is individual. The key is to find for each child what works for them. Many of the ideas below will need the child's consent, but it is not difficult to ask:

- watch a burning candle
- walk on the beach, listen to waves crashing
- gaze at the night sky: moons, stars, shooting stars
- walk in the countryside, hearing, smelling and touching nature
- paint nails, or fix nail extensions
- use essential oils or incense sticks
- listen to favourite music
- take a bubble bath
- brush your hair slowly and gently

- listen to a babbling brook, rain falling, or the wind rustling the leaves of trees
- listen to talk radio to hear human voices
- hug someone you trust
- soak your feet
- use perfumed skin creams or lotions
- put clean sheets on the bed
- stroke a pet
- have a soothing drink such as hot milk, tea or hot chocolate (be careful with caffeine)
- use a favourite scent
- hug a pillow or a soft toy
- sink into a really comfortable chair
- curl up under a fleecy blanket
- have a head or hand massage
- rub your hands with fragrant, creamy lotion
- put a cold compress on your forehead
- light a scented candle
- walk in a scented garden.

## THE PHYSICAL ENVIRONMENT

Although the physical environment may be the easiest aspect of the planned environment to arrange, it still needs to be thought about from the same perspective as the other elements, taking account of the inner world of the child and what it is that we are communicating symbolically to them. The physical environment should be a symbolic representation of the therapeutic process.

The home's location, design and size should meet the needs of the children, support each child's development and enable them to lead as normal a life as possible and take account of each child's individual care needs and privacy. To this end, the adults need to be actively involved in maintaining a well-designed and pleasant home environment, using the available space to meet their needs.

The home should be clean, warm, comfortable, welcoming, cared for and homely. It is not necessary, or even desirable, that everything should be new, or the very best quality. New things easily show damage, and cost does need to be thought about. But furnishing and fittings should convey to the child the message that they have nice things in their home because they, the child, are of value. Resourcefulness and imagination in furnishing and equipping the home are good lessons for children to learn.

Things will get damaged from the child's low emotional regulation and their habits. Damage is not a personal attack on us as caregivers, and we need to be good at not reacting impulsively or angrily. All behaviour is a form of communication and our first task is to try and understand what the child is trying to tell us. The child may never have been looked after, and perhaps cannot look after themself. It is not surprising that they cannot look after their home. Damages should be repaired quickly, perhaps with the child's help as part of making restitution, and broken items should be removed and replaced promptly. Damage and breakages that are left without repair act as a constant reinforcer of the child's internal working model, and convey the message to the child that the adults either cannot manage to maintain their environment, or do not care.

The physical environment should have appropriate emphasis on safety; medicines and poisons (e.g. substances hazardous to health) and sharp items are securely stored and their whereabouts known. However, unless there is a specific risk, it is not therapeutic to lock away all low-toxicity substances (like shampoo or perfume) in the name of safety, as this creates an unreal sense of danger, and promotes an over-controlling environment, where children have to ask adults for everything.

It is helpful to be able to secure the external doors. The child needs to be fully confident that strangers and past abusers cannot get in. By the same token, visitors should be explicitly monitored and vetted.

Windows should have curtains or blinds, and it is helpful if there is a predictable routine over when these are closed. Closing them at dusk, or before the evening meal, signals that the focus is now inside the house, as night approaches. A sense of place and of belonging is encouraged by displaying photographs of the child and their peers, and photographs of the adults, and by displaying their artwork and school projects. There should be toys and activities that allow the child to play at both their developmental level and their chronological age, and adults should avoid commenting when the child selects either.

Arts, crafts and other creative activities are always useful, and a well-stocked craft box, with pens, glue, paper, recycled household items, stickers, glitter and much, much more, has saved many a child and adult from boredom, and allowed imaginative expression of the child's inner world as a positive alternative to acting out.

It is important to distinguish between the private and the shared space in the home. Explicit boundaries between public and private space give a clear message about appropriate personal boundaries, and help children in group settings feel they have a place that is safe from the acted-out anguish of peers.

A child's room should be individualized, but the public spaces represent the group, in which each individual's preferences are valued, but none dominate. As a child becomes more autonomous, their room can become an important space in which to be independent and free of adult interference. Children should be encouraged and supported to personalize their rooms as well as contributing their ideas to the décor, planning and use of the shared spaces.

Letting the child choose their bedding encourages them to enjoy going to bed. Bedside lights, which may need to be left on all night, soften a room and create a relaxed feeling at bedtime. A desk and bookcase give the child somewhere for homework. Sitting on the child's bed may not feel safe, and a bedroom chair gives you somewhere to sit while you read a story. Windows are often best covered with a net as well as curtains, so that the space can feel contained even during the day. A hallway light lights the way to the bathroom during the dark hours and also reminds the child that you are still holding them in mind while you sleep.

Many highly anxiously attached children endlessly rearrange their furniture. This can present problems for adults, but the child is establishing a sense of control, attempting to create their own order out of chaos, and processing their thoughts and feelings. Aside from legitimate concerns for safety (which do need to be addressed) children do better if adults are fairly relaxed about this.

The child's bedroom is their private space and in most circumstances should only be entered with the child's permission. However, this should not lead to neglecting the child who cannot care for themself properly. If caregivers need to help, they may need to insist that they do so, explaining to the child that they are doing so until the child does not need their assistance. This should all be undertaken in the spirit of consent and collaboration, not as a power struggle.

The same care needs to be taken outside the home. A garden is almost essential, although it is possible to provide a therapeutic environment without one. Boundary fences and hedges need to be clear and well maintained, as they symbolize the boundaries that we are trying to provide. The best gardens are equipped with play equipment, places to skate and ride bikes, to run and hide and sit quietly. It is easy to develop a small sensory garden for quiet reflection. Something to hit and swing on and jump and scream provides a release for unregulated emotion, without the need to break and damage and destroy inside the house.

## FOUR PHASES OF PLACEMENT

It is helpful to have a clear sense of what the task is at each point in the child's stay. It is confusing if adults are unclear what expectations it is reasonable to have of a child, yet there are often competing and contradictory demands. This tension can be resolved if there is clarity about task, and so unpacking and developing the practice skills that workers require for each stage of placement is key to this work. The four-phase model of recovery presented here is adapted from the widely accepted three-stage model of trauma recovery (see Cairns 2002 and Sutton 2007) by adding Transition, as all young people in care will make a transition either to another form of formal looking after, or to independence. The stages are Stabilization, Integration, Adaptation and Transition.

The child's levels of emotional arousal will fluctuate through each phase (see Figure 2.1). Predictably, they will be hyper-aroused upon placement, due in part to the stress of a change. This stress will be higher if the move is unwanted or unplanned and the child is not involved, consulted and prepared. The main task of stabilization is to reduce the child's arousal, so that they can begin to feel safe in a predictable world.

During the integration phase, arousal levels may fluctuate wildly, and adults need to be skilled at both challenging the child and soothing them. Later, the child's general arousal levels will be lower, and the focus becomes adapting to the world beyond. However, as the child nears the end of their placement, their arousal once again will rise.

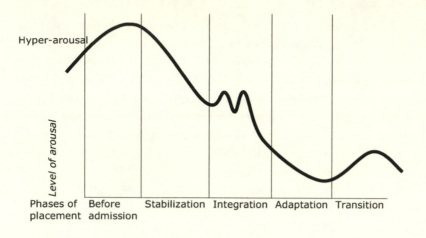

Figure 2.1: Arousal through the phases of placement

## Phase 1: Stabilization

The first phase in recovery is to provide a safe haven/secure base and establish a strong therapeutic alliance based on trust. This allows the child to develop the capacity for self-protection, self-soothing and self-care. Arousal is high, so the emphasis is on a low-arousal, containing environment in which adults set and maintain the emotional tone. The process is through developing relationships that the child experiences as trustworthy and predictable. Of course, this takes time. The child needs to be thought about all the time, and their needs met in a predictable way. Adults need to be able to think about the child's overt behaviour in terms of expressions of unmet primary needs, and focus on meeting these needs more than changing the behaviour. We should also remember that the child needs us to stick to promises and commitments, to build trust, and to tell the truth consistently to reduce fear.

The child may need to return to a process of stabilization many times. In some way, they may never be beyond this phase; deeply disturbing and highly vulnerable children may always require stabilizing. Change is frightening for the child because it requires relinquishing deeply embedded defences. Before they are able to bear this process, they need to learn to feel safe in their developmental niche, where they will begin to relinquish their solitary coping.

## Readiness milestones

Before thinking about moving on to the next phase, integration, which needs the child's trust and co-operation, it is important to consider their readiness. Below is a suggestion, adapted from Sutton's (2007) work on trauma recovery, of some of the skills that a child or young person needs to have acquired in order to face the next difficult phase. They may not have all these, but they need enough. Some of the work of stabilization can be to prepare and provide these milestones:

- I feel comfortable enough to be able to talk to someone about how difficult my life is.

- I have things I can do instead of hurting myself or other people, or damaging property.

- I have a safe place to go if I need to leave the house, and I will return.

- I am able to feel uncomfortable, scared and frustrated.

- I am able to think about acting out without having to actually do so.

## Phase 2: Integration

The next phase follows once safety has been established. Although much of the work of Phase 1 continues, Phase 2 is significantly different. The child has developed a secure base and understands trusting relationships with reliable adults as a safe haven. The adult's task is to allow the child to develop a coherent account of their early experiences. The child can now begin to acquire earned security through exploring contradictory thoughts and feelings from their early relationships and unravelling feelings of self-blame, shame and guilt from the reality that they did not receive care that was good enough, overcoming their denial or disbelief.

They can grieve for the inevitable losses (lost childhood, loss of safety and trust, letting go of false beliefs about people from the past, etc.) and be encouraged and supported to piece together their traumatic story, often through non-verbal means (painting, writing, drawing, music, poetry, rap, drama), with the eventual goal that their story is verbalized.

During stabilization the holding environment is closely woven around the child. The child's disruption, which expresses the poor integration between thoughts and feelings, and easily spills out into their home, is strongly contained. During the second phase, disruption is seen as an opportunity to work towards integrating the child's inner turmoil. Although maintaining safety and stability remains important, caregivers are able to take some of the child's disruptive behaviour as an opportunity to work more imaginatively with the child's inner world, using tools such as creativity, explanation, play and reflection, to explore with the child. In a group setting, this can only happen if the group of adults who may need to contain the child's emotions are prepared and equipped to do so, so it is important to consider a range of factors including: other stressors, the time of day, the emotional state of the group, group dynamics, the skills and experience of the staff group at that time. As in all aspects of therapeutic care, communication is crucial. It is essential to make decisions and to act upon them, and reflect and learn from them later.

At times, this work can feel unsafe for the child and for the adults. Powerful feelings need to be processed and integrated. The child may return to earlier risk-taking behaviours to defend against contradictory and confusing feelings, and so it is often necessary to revisit Phase 1 many times.

## Phase 3: Adaptation

With a degree of earned security and a developing coherent account of their attachment history, the child recognizes the role-differentiated nature of relationships and moves from the almost complete dependence of earlier phases towards autonomy and interdependence. The adult's task is to support the child to acquire and practise an increasing range of social skills in a widening social environment, in order to reconnect with ordinary life; developing a new sense of self, forming new relationships, experiencing a sense of power, control and self-esteem, and acquiring protective skills for the future. Clubs, social activities, and other ways of accessing same-age peer groups (perhaps a return to mainstream schooling, etc.) provide these opportunities. The child will still require our scaffolding and support, and may at times revert to former coping strategies under the stress of coping with these new experiences.

## Phase 4: Transition

If the child has acquired a degree of earned security, developed some autonomy and integrated thoughts and feelings, transition is a positive experience. However, the child will also experience a sense of loss as they begin to recognize that they will be moving on from valued and needed relationships. They may also be daunted by the loss of the scaffolding and support that they are facing. They may need help adapting to these feelings. Their feelings are validated by caregivers acknowledging that the price of caring is to feel loss on separation. As always, the child needs us to be truthful.

With any transition, self-esteem may suffer, and the child may once again revert to earlier ways of coping. They may need to create rejection in us in order to break the attachment bond. Our task is to let go whilst protecting the security of the child's relationship with us. We need to be real with the child about the challenges ahead, and how much support we will be able to provide. This phase has most chance of success if the current placement and the new can work together, and the child or young person is involved in choices and decision-making.

## Therapeutic relationships over time

Neither distant nor involved, it is the caregiver's engaged self within the therapeutic relationship that makes the difference, provides the support and genuinely cares about the child. There is a significant shift in the nature of the supportive relationship over time that reflects the four phases of placement.

Initially, the child may not recognize the sensitive availability of the caring adults, as their internal working model of caregivers is as hostile, interfering, unavailable and rejecting. Therefore we need to endlessly find creative ways to express sensitive availability in the face of the child's hostile dependency or extreme withdrawal. The child needs some reliable and trusted relationships for the work of integration, and may draw closer to some caregivers than others. We should respect this, whilst being open to the idea of these dynamics changing.

As some degree of integration between thoughts and feelings is achieved, and the work moves into adaptation and transition, the child is more able to trust the adults, and now needs some control over triggering their availability. As caregivers allow this shift from highly proactive availability to a more reactive stance, the child experiences greater self-efficacy and a growing sense of autonomy.

## ORGANIZATIONAL VALUES AND ETHOS

A planned environment needs to be sustained by a wider organizational structure that reflects the ethos, values and ways of relatedness caregivers provide for the children. A therapeutic approach can only be sustained if caregivers are supported and valued, and if the organization provides suitable resources relevant to the placement phase for each child. A key aspect of this support is supervision.

## Supervision

Supervision is a central tool to delivering organizational support for a therapeutic environment. However, it is not infrequently stated that the demands of the work make this impossible to arrange. But, if the work is so demanding, is it not essential to find the time for the support and guidance that supervision provides?

When regular and effective supervision is not happening, an important first step is to ensure that it happens frequently. Monthly supervision that lasts between one and a half to two hours is probably the minimum useful amount. Committing to meeting regularly will provide clear task and structure. To know who is doing what, and roughly what they are doing, is in itself an important change. Those who wish to avoid supervision no longer can; those who wish to make use of it are given the opportunity to do so. Over time, a cultural shift emerges. Initially, workers may approach supervision with trepidation; their experience not infrequently mirrors the child's primary experiences of abuse or neglect: being micro-managed, blamed and let down, or else being abandoned.

However, when workers and their line managers use supervision well, it provides an essential element to the holding environment: holding and containing the anxieties and the work of the staff. For this process to begin supervisor and supervisee need to understand that, just as for the child, the adult's current experience is most effectively understood with some reference to their inner world, their early experiences and their mental processes. When focusing on the work with the young people, it is helpful to ask two questions: What are the distinct characteristics of my helping relationship with this child? How does this compare with my other relationships?

Supervision covers four functions that need to be reconciled to each other, as contradictions and tensions exist between them. These functions can be summarized as:

- personal support
- training, education and development

- problem-solving and analysis
- workload management and accountability.

Clearly there is a possible conflict in, for example, the personal support function, where the feelings and difficulties of the work are shared, and the accountability function, where task completion and work quality are the focus. Recognizing possible tensions between these functions, and having an explicit agreement that they will be thought about as discrete from each other, allows both parties to feel safe. Supervision is helped if both parties understand these four functions, and how, although at times they may overlap, they represent discrete areas that should not bleed into each other.

### The starting point of effective supervision

- Supervision happens on time and appointments are booked, no excuses. Supervisors also get regular supervision.

- Supervision agreements are made between both parties. The purpose, process and boundaries are explicit, and even though they change and develop, they always need to be made explicit.

- Both parties draw up agendas.

- Supervisors receive training and the management group problem-solves for individual managers: individual work issues are seen as the management group's concern more than individual manager's.

- The manager has authority and the worker is valued and given a true voice in their supervision. Managers acknowledge that the workers contain the powerful feelings of the child, and their role is to hold and contain the powerful feelings of the workers.

- Trust takes time to develop and has to be earned. Trust is earned by delivering on commitments and avoiding blame.

- Practice-led managers reflect their practice with the children in their supervision model, and apply psychodynamic understanding that stresses that there are unconscious as well as conscious elements to our interactions.

- Supervision recognizes team members' interdependence upon each other and that the team and individuals need nurturing and leadership.

- A work culture exists that gives appropriate autonomy, clarity of task, proper support, acceptance of mistakes, mutual and reciprocal problem-solving, clear accountability, and acknowledgement of necessary and appropriate power.

- Unhealthy relationship roles are understood, acknowledged and unpacked. Nobody is permitted to operate as victim, rescuer or persecutor without this being challenged.

- Managers are accessible to supervisees at other times, building and sustaining a culture of value, trust and respect.

## THERAPEUTIC RISK

Risk is an unavoidable part of life, and children need opportunities to experience some danger in order to learn how to accurately assess risk for themselves. We rightly place a great deal of emphasis on safeguarding, but can often become risk adverse. Over-controlling and coercive responses are frequently driven by a poorly conducted risk assessment. Sometimes short-term risks need to be taken for long-term gains. Total risk avoidance is known to lead to over-restriction, which can in itself be damaging to an individual's welfare and to therapeutic relationships. Sometimes it is necessary to take reasoned risks to achieve therapeutic gain (Department of Health 2007).

Risk assessment attempts to predict the onset, continuity or escalation of a risk based on reasonably stable personal characteristics and environmental circumstances. Risk management is a creative and dynamic process that uses information gathered through a thorough risk assessment to understand and manage predisposing factors, triggers, strengths and protective factors, Risk is most simply understood as a calculation between how likely it is that an event will occur, and how much harm will be caused if it does occur. All things may be possible, but what we need to consider is how probable an event is. If we focus on the amount of harm without sensibly considering how probable the event is, the child becomes insulated from all possible harm, but does not develop the ability to make their own judgements about risk.

Risk with a high probability of occurrence and a high probability of harm requires robust risk management plans, that focus on reducing probability and harm. However, risks with low probability of occurring that result in high harm if they do may be more effectively managed by focusing on reducing harm, and it may be necessary that efforts to reduce the probability of the event occurring may be wasted, since the probability of it occurring is low. In contrast, high-probability risks with little harm may present ideal learning opportunities for young people, and, as well as measures to reduce the probability, this can be reflected in a risk management plan. Low-harm, low-probability risks may be acceptable with little management, allowing young people to experience a sensible level of risk, and avoiding risk aversion. A suitable format for considering this process of risk assessment might follow Table 2.1.

**Table 2.1: Risk assessment and management framework**

| Risk | Probability | Harm | Strategies | Strategies | Managed |
|---|---|---|---|---|---|
| Describe the nature of the risk. | How likely is the risk to occur? | What harm is done to the young person or others if the risk occurs? | What strategies are in place to manage the probability of the risk occurring? | What strategies are in place to reduce the harm? | Is the risk satisfactorily managed? |

When considering risk, it is also important to consider protective factors within the child; to what extent does the child possess qualities, or have in their environment factors that make them less vulnerable to risks? Protective factors would usually be seen as such things as:

- good self-help skills
- healthy self-esteem
- positive self-image
- intelligence
- good communication skills
- confidence
- positive values
- supportive peer groups
- interests
- ambition
- impulse control

- sociability

- social integration.

Risk assessment and management plans should be shared with all involved. It is particularly important that agreement to the various judgements is gained from everybody with parental responsibility. Most importantly, share the risk assessment with the young person; they may well be unaware of the impact of their behaviour on themselves or others.

Risk assessment and management is an ongoing process. Every incident can confirm that risks are correctly assessed and adequately managed or that changes need to be made. Keep others informed of any changes. The process can allow the individual's core beliefs and habitual behaviours to be challenged, and help identify skills that can be learned in therapy or therapeutic relationships.

## SMOOTHING TRANSITIONS

A transition presents a potentially difficult time for any of us. For children who have experienced multiple unplanned and unwanted changes, the whole experience of change and transition can be frightening and unwelcome, and can awaken feelings of loss and abandonment. They may have well-developed coping mechanisms to help them deal with the cognitive and emotional turmoil that is associated with change. Peers, caregivers or teachers may well not welcome these coping mechanisms, but, although they do not work well in any adaptive way, they probably work quite well for the child, in that they keep them from re-experiencing their traumatic memories.

Whilst we need to consider our response to these coping mechanisms, we are primarily concerned here with how we can manage the small daily transitions that each child experiences every day. By managing the process of transition effectively we help the child escape from a cycle of negative experiences that habitually surround change. These negative cycles reinforce the child's view of themselves as unworthy, as failures and as un-helpable. By proactively managing transitions for the child we make ourselves consistently available to their needs, engendering a growing sense of trust, and provide a form of emotional scaffolding that supports the child as they internalize a set of new responses, that are better adjusted to family life and society. Preparation is one way to help mitigate unsettling effects of transitions. Most people cope well with change when it is predictable, expected and planned. This is more likely to happen if we have recognized transitions as happening and have some insight into the difficulty change can present to insecure children. Good beginnings and good endings are also important as they maintain a sense of structure. Let the child know how an event will end and what will follow. (For example: when going on a walk, telling the child what will happen when they return, what they, you and other people will be doing.) Knowing the child helps smooth transitions, knowing what works best for each child in managing their anxieties over transitions, and what doesn't work. In group settings particularly, it can help to plan ahead; perhaps transitions can be staggered. It may be easier to support a child through a transition if others in the group are more settled. Staff need to be clear about who is doing what.

## WAYS OF CAREGIVING

The planned environment symbolically represents a secure base. It promotes proximity to safe, predictable and consistent caregivers by arranging the socio-emotional environment as a child-centred developmental niche in which the child is safely held and contained. This requires structure, planning and support, and provides a therapeutic frame in which genuine, engaged relationships are supported and protected. In the next chapter we turn to ways of caregiving within the therapeutic frame.

## Chapter Three

# Ways of Caregiving

## Working Within the Therapeutic Frame

Humans are social creatures and group living is an essential aspect of the way children are cared for and protected until they are sufficiently independent to survive. In most cases this group is the family, although clearly, what a family is varies across time and cultures. Children in public care have been taken from at least one group setting that has not sufficiently met their needs and been placed in others. Therapeutic care provides the child with the experience of living in a functional group where relationships with adults in a parenting role are healthy: a normative experience that may undo what the child has learnt in less functional groups.

## LEARNING OUTCOMES FOR THIS CHAPTER

Once you have studied this chapter you should be able to:

- provide good enough care
- employ the engaged self in the therapeutic encounter
- promote the child's mental capacity to consider others' minds
- promote healthy self-esteem
- provide authoritative parenting
- help the child overcome lagging problem-solving social skills
- promote reintegration following shame-inducing experiences
- reflect on the emotional labour of the work and seek adequate support
- recognize and respond to unhealthy relationship roles
- promote positive and regulated experiences
- apply explicit boundaries and manage consequences therapeutically
- deal effectively with power struggles.

## GOOD ENOUGH PARENTING

The term 'good enough parenting' indicates that a secure development does not require perfection on the caregiver's behalf. The essential thing is that the infant's needs are sufficiently met. Most infants have a good enough experience, the basis for healthy emotional development. Good enough parenting includes:

- consistency

- adequate stimulation

- appropriate affection

- pride in the child's achievements and development

- expectation that the child will behave in a way that is appropriate to their age and development.

The good enough parent attempts to understand the child's emotional and cognitive states, and interacts with a distressed infant by calming, soothing and reassuring, providing proximity in response to separation distress. The child learns to trust the safety provided by the attachment figure and recognizes that their emotions are manageable, can be contained, and will not overwhelm them.

However, parenting that falls below the baseline jeopardizes the emotional health of the child, and a deficit in early experience needs to be recovered by receiving a degree of emotional support that far exceeds that required by a same-age child with a secure attachment. Carers need to be able to respond not just to the child's current needs, but also to layers of unmet need from early childhood and the fear of abandonment that is an insecure attachment.

## HOPEFULNESS

Hope for positive change is an essential factor in therapeutic work generally, and a realistic hopefulness and a focus on the possibility of change are important aspects of the therapeutic relationship. Traumatized children need to achieve hope that change is possible. The child may initially be highly resistant to help, fearing the loss of their tried and trusted defences. The quality of their involvement in their care is highly dependent on the warmth and friendliness displayed by carers, who therefore need to be 'hopeful role models' for the child needing help, establishing trust through consistent respect, courtesy, warmth, and optimism that the child can work towards their recovery.

## THE ENGAGED SELF: WHY DOING IS BETTER THAN TALKING

Therapeutic work requires that we bring ourselves in the relationship to establish a therapeutic alliance. However, as mistrust of adults is deeply internalized, this raises conflict between levels of warmth and friendliness versus control. Whilst we may wish that the child would see their problems the way we do, that is unlikely; helpfulness and protection offered by the adult are likely to be heavily defended against by the child. Attitudes displayed by carers towards the child are key elements in building a therapeutic alliance with the child. An empathic, non-judgemental approach is essential. The caregiver becomes engaged by being actively involved with the child, enhancing mutual understanding and making a connection through action. It is more effective to get participation by initiating or helping than by telling. For example, we are more likely to bring the child to participate with us by starting to straighten out their bed than if we insist, 'This bed must be remade!' In remaking the bed together we join in mutual interaction that is positive and builds relationship.

The use of precise language is very important when communicating with traumatized children. The skilled caregiver develops a sense of communication difficulty that is embedded in disruptive and challenging behaviours, and in response to this cultivates a careful form of working that allows them to empathetically communicate through the child's distress and demonstrate attunement towards them, through acceptance, curiosity and empathy. The constant reassurance that insecurely attached children need can be woven into scripts that reaffirm this empathetic understanding, and defuse their ability to draw adults into conflict-laden stimulus-response scenarios.

By being engaged, we promote the importance of the adult–child relationship. Interaction, responsiveness, and reciprocity are important factors in relatedness to others. By offering activities that include adventure, variety, stimulation, and novelty, a child can understand that surprises can be fun and new experiences with others can be enjoyable. The child learns that there is more for them in a relationship than in their defended isolation. Close proximity gets beyond the child's insecure attachment and defensiveness.

## MIND-MINDEDNESS

Children are born needing to be part of a family and a culture. They strive to understand the world by sharing experiences. Infants' earliest interactions involve taking an active part in developing shared understanding with caregivers, fitting their own subjective experiences to the caregiver's subjective consciousness. This intersubjectivity is the process that makes it possible for individuals to understand and change each other's minds and behaviour. It is achieved through recognition and co-ordination of intentions in caregiver–infant pairs. The capacity for social understanding grows out of this intersubjectivity. It is the ability to see how things might look for another person, and is the basis of empathy, relationship skills, and moral behaviour. Empathy and mutual mind-mindedness are essential for both psychological development and social competence.

The child's mental capacity to consider what is in the mind of their caregivers is promoted when parental figures have a well-developed capacity to think about the contents of their own and others' minds, and is more likely to develop secure attachment. In contrast, individuals with attachment difficulty have a diminished capacity to form representations of their caretakers' inner thoughts and feelings, as they defensively protect themself from having to recognize the wish to harm them that may be present in the mind of the attachment figure. This diminished capacity to have mental representations of the feelings and thoughts of self and others accounts for many of the core symptoms of emotional disturbance, including an unstable sense of self, impulsivity, and chronic feelings of emptiness.

Mind-minded caregivers are good at translating the child's psychological experiences into an active, coherent dialogue that helps achieve security of attachment and facilitates emotional understanding. By the caregiving adult choosing to focus on the child as an individual with a mind and their own subjective experiences, rather than an entity with needs to be met, the child learns how to understand their own inner states, which lays the foundation for mental well-being. Mind-mindedness involves keeping the child aware of the cognitive components of their experience. It can be introduced into the way we talk to children. When we ask, during peek-a-boo games 'Who do you *think* that is?' rather than 'Who is that in there? Is it you?' and when the child asks us, 'What is such and such?' and we reply, 'Tell me what you *think* it is,' we are being mind-minded.

## SELF-ESTEEM

Of all social concepts, the self is most basic. It enables the individual to adopt a stance from which to view the world. Self-esteem is an individual's feeling of his or her own worthiness, a self-evaluative system that is related to the image of an ideal self that we all have. Self-esteem is sometimes understood as a single global entity, but can also be seen as specific to a number of domains of behaviour, each of which an individual may feel differently about. Harter (1987) distinguished between five domains: scholastic competence, athletic competence, social acceptance, physical appearance, and behavioural conduct. The gap between how important it was for a child to do well in each domain, and how well they believe they do can be seen as a measure of self-esteem in each domain. Children's self-esteem can vary considerably from one domain to another.

Individuals value the people around them according to how they value themselves. Thus, an individual with a low self-worth will find it difficult to respond to others as if they are of any value. Since their need for belonging and love is not being satisfied, they will be unable to satisfy this need in anyone else. But even individuals with a healthy self-esteem may be less able to respond in a positive way than usual when in pain or discomfort or ill. It is also important to recognize that past experience can have an effect. If an individual has experienced betrayal and untrustworthiness then it would be surprising if they were ready to trust again. Being valued and becoming able to value themselves is an essential aspect of secure base experiences.

### Self-esteem: the gap between selves

Children also have a generalized feeling of self-worth that is not tied up to any specific domain. This emerges later, once a child is able to assess themselves independently of any activity (about age seven or eight). When there is little discrepancy between the ideal self and the perceived real self (between the idealized image of ourselves and what we perceive ourselves to be) an individual experiences high self-esteem. If the discrepancy is great, an individual experiences low self-esteem.

Healthy self-esteem is built upon a realistic sense of both the ideal self and the perceived real self, and goes up and down within limits.

Healthy self-esteem requires a sense of place and connectedness to our personal history and warmth, value and security. Children who do not live at home often believe it is their fault. This alone is enough to seriously damage their self-esteem. If they are the victims of emotional, physical or sexual abuse, their self-esteem could well be destroyed.

The self-esteem of any child growing up away from their own family is vulnerable to their having no sense of belonging in a family. Caregivers need to help the child develop a comfortable sense of belonging in two places, by finding ways to include the child socially and personally in their living group and helping the child feel an appropriate sense of connectedness and belonging to their birth family.

Belonging can be demonstrated on a practical level, but it also requires unconditional positive regard and the reassurance of practical and emotional support. Well-planned and adequately supported family contact can help a child not lose touch with their place in their family. Valuing parents and developing effective partnerships enables the child to see their difficulties in the context in which they arose. When substitute caregivers treat birth parents with respect and value, the child feels valued and able to belong in their birth family. But we must also be honest with the child about their future in their birth family, or the child may retreat to defensive fantasies about their family.

When we have low self-esteem we are likely to misunderstand and misinterpret those around us, seeing everything as a threat. We are likely to be short tempered and pessimistic. And the child with low self-esteem is likely to project their low value of themselves outwards at us.

If time in foster or residential care has one satisfactory outcome, it must be that children leave with a greater sense of their own worth than they joined us, and as professionals working in this field, we must carefully watch every response to ensure that we do not contribute to either their low opinion, or a narcissistically inflated opinion of themselves. This must be genuine. Children are not without self-awareness and they resent false praise and are likely to be demotivated by it. Nothing is likely to motivate a child more than genuine, empathetic praise. Even giving tangible rewards for achievements has been shown to be of questionable benefit. Praise is most effective in building self-esteem when it is couched in terms of effort rather than ability. It is better to say, 'You've done really well, I can see you've made a lot of effort', than 'You've done really well, you're very good at this'.

The reason for this is that praise that focuses on internal qualities rather than the effort the child has made can leave the child unsure if they have the capacity to perform in that way again, whereas praising effort means that the child knows they can try to achieve. Praise that is given too generously for any small achievement, or in an attempt to boost self-esteem, tends to promote a kind of narcissism in the child, a potentially dangerous sense that whatever they do is praiseworthy.

## Influence of parenting

Self-esteem is influenced by parental attitudes. Parents with good self-esteem themselves, who set clear limits on the child's behaviour, but show high acceptance of the child and their behaviours, and allow considerable freedom within these limits encourage healthy self-esteem. In contrast, parenting that is distant, rejecting, autocratic or over-permissive, damages self-esteem. Of course, children may experience parenting from foster parents or residential workers that boosts self-esteem and parenting from birth families that diminishes it. This is another example of the way in which the abandoned and traumatized child gets caught by the dilemma of their lived experience.

And there is much that we can do to genuinely boost a child's self-esteem, providing safety, belonging and unconditional positive regard, as well as information about and connection with the child's past, for example through Life Story Work.

## PARENTING STYLES

Therapeutic parenting proceeds by bothering, where nobody has before, by treating with respect, gaining consent and earning and giving trust, by being truthful in the face of the child's unrealities, by giving support without creating dependency, by giving permission for the expression of overwhelming feelings, and through socialization into acceptable social values. We bring our relationship inheritance with us (although we may not always be aware of this), and part of this inheritance is our experiences of the (family) groups in which we have lived. These often unknown or unspoken assumptions guide the interactions that the carer brings into the relationship. Caregivers are helped to work within a therapeutic frame if an effective, predictable and consistent parenting style is developed. This does not provide a series of situation-specific solutions to difficulties, but provides caregivers with a frame that allows them to develop a predictable, therapeutic response to each situation as it arises, promoting their autonomy and confidence, and allowing the developing relationship to be genuine.

Parenting styles have varying outcomes for children: with weak parenting skills a child may become non-compliant and enter an escalating cycle of parent–child conflict where growing negative attention is compounded by a failure to reward positive behaviour, but with sufficient skill, troubled children can be re-parented. Parenting styles can be seen as a continuum, from authoritarian at one extreme, to chaotic at the other (Figure 3.1).

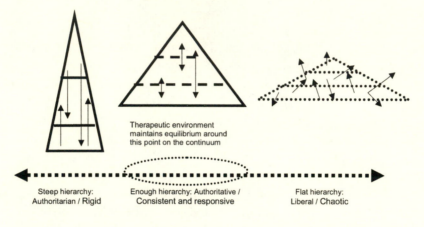

Figure 3.1: Continuum of parenting styles

Overly liberal parenting sets few boundaries and tends not to guide children through their development, believing that children will develop spontaneously through a process of maturation. In this style of parenting children are often not distinguished from adults. They have rights, but no responsibilities. There are few, if any, clear boundaries, rules, roles or expectations: anything goes. Power rests with whoever grabs it. There are few expectations, and aspirations are often low. Extremes of this parenting style correlate with anxious-avoidant attachment; children may be neglected and under-stimulated. Self-esteem is damaged by the hidden message that the child is worthless.

Authoritarian parenting is very child directive. Powerful group members hold all the power. Weaker members are disempowered at all levels. Children have responsibilities, but no rights. Authoritarian parenting is over-burdened by rules, and driven by punishment and blame. Children are treated as less important and less valuable than adults. At its extreme children may be physically and emotionally abused. Although parental corporal punishment may be associated with high levels of immediate compliance, it is also closely associated with the development of aggression in the child, and lower levels of moral internalization and mental health: even if it works to stop children misbehaving, it damages their development, their life chances and their moral growth, and can lead to anxious-resistant attachment. It damages the child's self-esteem with the message that the child is inadequate. Most damaging is an unpredictable mix, inconsistent or chaotic parenting. The child does not know which response their behaviour will elicit; they may be blamed or praised, wanted or rejected. It is inconsistent, unpredictable parenting that most damages children. Boundaries are blurred and changeable, as are expectations, explanations and consequences. Children are at risk of physical, emotional and sexual abuse, and developing insecure, disorganized attachment.

In contrast to these parenting styles, authoritative parenting acknowledges that adults are the authority in the group, but all group members are empowered. Children have rights and responsibilities appropriate to their level of development. Children are seen as worthwhile. They are consulted and listened to and their rights are respected, but there is still a clear distinction between children and adults based on recognition of learning and development achieved. Children feel safe and can develop to their full potential, learn to trust others and develop empathy. There is appropriate discipline that helps a child to meet expectations, in contrast to more punitive approaches which are there to alleviate adult frustration.

Authoritative parenting provides a consistent and predictable, emotionally rich, and clearly bounded developmental niche, holding the child in mind and providing care and control. It does not mean over-protecting the child from real world experiences; it does mean providing sufficient emotional support for the child to survive real world challenges. Children need the adult to be an authority in their lives, but in contrast to being authoritarian, authoritative parenting can be summarized as demonstrating high expectations, providing good explanation, and showing genuine warmth.

High expectations place limits and controls on the child, and encourage independence. They demonstrate value and respect, and encourage the child to think beyond their low opinion of themselves. Carers need to empathetically acknowledge that they are expecting a lot, and that this may be hard for the child, but let them know they are fully confident they can and will meet those expectations.

Good explanation gives the reasons behind the rules; it guides rather than leads. The child has opportunity to understand why things happen, but this does not imply that everything is open to negotiation. Young people deserve proper explanation, which demonstrates value and respect, and by taking time to explain to the child, caregivers begin to build co-operation and consent. It is important to consider the child's developmental and functional level and pitch explanation appropriately, carefully considering communication style, picking a time when the child is receptive, and avoiding nagging.

All humans require warmth, without it we cannot thrive. Genuine warmth is provided through nurture. It is seen in genuine interest and attention, and in honest praise and encouragement. Warmth can be communicated through facial expressions, body language and appropriate touch, and in a warm, welcoming physical environment. Warmth demonstrates value and respect, and develops co-operation and consent. Warmth should not be withdrawn as a punishment; the child needs the experience of repair and reattunement following shame-inducing experiences. Caregivers can use warmth even when tackling problems: 'It's because we care what you do that we're keeping you in tonight'. Self-esteem is enhanced by two clear messages: expectations – 'you can do it', and warmth – 'you are cared about'. The benefits of the authoritative model are summarized in Table 3.1.

The task is to maintain equilibrium around the central model of the authoritative parent. However, powerful forces exist to push this process off course. This continuum is also a useful way of thinking about the organizational structure and management styles around our own work. In order for frontline staff to be held safely to work therapeutically with the child, they need to be supported and guided in an authoritative manner that mirrors the appropriate balance between care and control that therapeutic care strives for. Relationships within the group and between different aspects of organizations need to be carefully monitored so that they too reflect a healthy group dynamic.

**Table 3.1: Benefits of the authoritative model**

| Authoritative professionals | Children learn |
|---|---|
| • balance being available, but not too available<br>• are child centred, but retain control<br>• give praise, but are honest<br>• show trust when trust is deserved<br>• give warmth whilst remaining professional<br>• develop empathy (not sympathy)<br>• listen to the child's beliefs and preferences<br>• stick to promises and commitments<br>• Criticise the action, not the child. | • that their uncontainable emotions can be safely contained, firstly by the adults, later by themselves<br>• that they are worthwhile and valued, able to give love and worthy of receiving it<br>• that their needs can be met<br>• to trust and to be trusted<br>• to respect and be respected<br>• to reach their full potential<br>• to one day be a good parent themselves. |

## PLANNING AUTHORITATIVE CARE

Consistent explanations and expectations are most likely if there is good communication. This is especially the case in group-care settings. Explanations also need to be carefully thought about. A written Individual Support and Development Plan (ISDP) is a useful tool to help promote consistency. One model is to begin with a timeline in order to identify expectations (which allows them to be made explicit to the child) and be clear about the explanation that backs up the expectation. We can then begin to map what happens when expectations are met, what happens when they are not met, and what is being done to support the child to meet the expectations. Although care needs to be taken not to create a rigid and inflexible regime, such an approach allows us to provide very high levels of consistency, even with relatively large groups of staff. In producing a plan like this it is essential that the expectations and explanations are backed up with engaged and genuine warmth.

Figure 3.2 is an excerpt from an example support plan, taken from a residential home, but in principle applicable to other settings. The plan is very individualized as it takes into account Ben's individual skills, achievements and wishes, and provides support where he experiences difficulty.

| Time | Event | Expectation | Explanation | If expectation is met? | If expectation is not met? | Support to meet expectation? |
|---|---|---|---|---|---|---|
| 07:00-07:45 | Ben gets up and goes to school with school peers on the school bus. | Ben gets up and leaves the house in time. He catches the bus and gets to school. | Ben has asked to go on the school bus. | Ben has travel time with friends and more independence. | Adults take Ben to school by car, leaving at 8.30. | Ben is woken by staff at 7:00. He is reminded that his friends are expecting him. He has a bus pass. |
| 18.00-18.30 | Evening meal. | Ben to sit and eat his meals in a sociable way. | Eating together is one thing we do regularly as a group. This helps us all to feel we belong here. | Reflected in reward system. | Escalating behaviour means that he will lose the privilege of an evening offsite activity. Record on reward system. | Staff engage children and support a good atmosphere. They remind Ben of their expectations and tell him what he needs to do, not telling him what he should not do. |

Figure 3.2: Excerpt from a residential individual support and development plan

## DISCIPLINE

Children develop strategies of non-compliance over the first five years of life as they struggle between autonomy and dependence. Initially, they adopt passive non-compliance, then acquire simple refusal, which is followed by direct defiance. As the child becomes cognitively more sophisticated, they will begin to use excuses, before offering bargains and eventually negotiation. Boundary pushing and non-compliance are important aspects of healthy child development, but reasonable limits are necessary and are welcomed by children, and effective discipline is an important aspect of therapeutic care. Parents attempt to socialize children to distinguish right from wrong and to act accordingly. When children know the boundaries adults are placing on their behaviour they can explore within the limits, safe in the knowledge that they are valued. A conscience develops as a result of internalization of these adult rules.

It is helpful to distinguish discipline, which is intended to help the child meet expectations, and punishment, which is mostly in place to alleviate adult frustrations. Discipline is an ongoing process, which emphasizes what a child should do. It helps children to change, and assumes that adults set an example. Its aim is to establish self-control.

In contrast, punishment is reactive to events and emphasizes what a child should not do. Punishment undermines independence because it insists on obedience, and its primary purpose is to provide a release for the adults.

Particular styles of parental discipline are associated with conscience development. When faced with difficult behaviours, understanding that they need to find ways of changing the child's behaviour, many parents and carers intuitively focus on addressing these behaviours directly, often through sanctions and rewards. Although individual behaviours may be influenced to some degree by such approaches, the underlying behavioural style is unlikely to be addressed. Indeed, a coercive, power-based approach is likely to feed the child's defiance. Punishment may alleviate adult frustration, but is unlikely to help a child behave well because they want to. Love-based discipline, by which parents withhold affection in order to exert discipline, is ultimately punitive because it means abandonment. Power-based discipline, by which parents use superior power, including physical punishment and withholding privileges, is seen in statements like 'do it because I tell you'. It leads not to fear of consequences, but to anger and resentment.

Authoritative discipline, however, appeals not to fear or anger, but to the child's understanding, and helps them meet expectations and generalize the rule that the adult is asking them to adhere to. The child appreciates that responsibility lies with them, and associates the moral message with the event, not with the adult authority figure, and so internalizes it more easily. Based on giving explanations, it provides the child with a cognitive rationale to behave in a certain way ('when you hit your sister you hurt her').

As adults exercising discipline, we bring our childhood experiences of discipline and punishment with us. It is helpful to look at some of those experiences and ask ourselves what happened to us when we were children. Were there consequences that came from our misdeeds? How did the authority figures in our childhood react? What did we think about this, and how did it make us feel? Did it modify our behaviour, and if so how?

Attachment theory allows us to reframe disturbing and challenging behaviours as having meaning for the child and provides a compass to navigate our interactions with the 'difficult to reach' child. In response to unmet early needs, children develop difficult and challenging behaviours that are effective at getting what the child wants, or avoiding what they don't want. Unable to communicate these unmet needs through language, the child resorts to actions to express feelings. When faced with non-compliance, adults may feel that they have only two choices, either to use punishment-based strategies (such as power-based or love-based discipline) in order to gain compliance, or to lower their expectations of what the child can achieve in order to avoid conflict. However, neither of these approaches is effective at the time, nor do they help a child develop self-control.

Using punishment-based strategies may prompt increasingly difficult behaviour as a power struggle develops, and either the adult or the child will have to eventually back down. Most of us have the skills to accept having another person's will imposed on us when there is no alternative, but the children we are considering in this book may well not have acquired these skills. By using power-based discipline we set their challenging behaviours in motion. Our response to this is likely to be more of what has not worked, and so the child who is least able to accept the imposition of adult will is the one who is most expected to comply.

Faced with this, adults can feel they have no alternative but to give in to the child. However, reducing expectations empowers the child to use challenging behaviour as a way of avoiding the expectations and demands of others, and can leave the child feeling powerful yet bad.

However, over time, authoritative discipline changes behaviour, although we do need to invest some time in the child, both at the time of challenging behaviour and over time (because change takes time). It is sometimes rejected by adults as being too time consuming, although the time used up by a child's problem behaviours does not diminish if the behaviour continues.

This authoritative approach to challenging behaviour recognizes that the difficulties are derived from two factors, a lack of skills within the child to cope with adult demands, and an unresolved problem. This insight is in itself useful, as it allows a greater understanding of the child's perspective and a more compassionate response to their difficulty and opens up the possibility of the child being taught the skills that they lack.

These behaviours are usually cyclical in nature, reaching a crisis, then disappearing while the child regroups, but re-emerging later because nothing has improved. If we are not able to intervene therapeutically we often find the child getting worse, as each episode reinforces their wrongly held view that they are worthless, unlovable, unwanted, and lacking self-efficacy.

The behaviours may become addictive as they represent the only release from their mental anguish and the overwhelming feelings that accompany it. Small and powerless, the child learns to exert some power; feeling unloved, they are able to experience that they are unlovable in the anger and rejection that they elicit in adults exasperated and demoralized by their behaviour.

Episodes of challenging behaviour represent an opportunity to re-parent the child and to contradict their heavily defended internal working model. To work therapeutically requires that we intervene in the cycle in a way that is sensitively attuned to the child's emotional and cognitive need at the time. The functions we carry out therefore need to be matched to the child's place in the cycle.

The child's behaviour needs to be challenged, but if we do so when they are coping as best they can with their own high arousal (anxiety, fear, traumatic memories, sense of worthlessness, unresolved loss, etc.) we introduce challenge at a time when the child cannot cope, and they will feel that they need to defend themselves even more. This is when we can support them by validating their feelings, and by keeping them safe. It is later, when the crisis has passed, that they can be, and must be, gently and compassionately challenged on their behaviour, allowed to reflect and repair, and allowed to feel accountable without being rejected.

In this way, both the child and the adult survive the cycle of behaviour without the relationship being damaged, and the child experiences the relationship as a secure base from which they can explore their emotional and cognitive unintegration and challenge their distorted thinking and skewed emotions that are implicit in the IWM. A platform is laid for the long-term work of promoting recovery.

Often, the window for challenging is initially very small. During the stabilization phase of placement, the child is unlikely to be able to bear the impact of their IWM being directly challenged. Later, in the integration phase, their reaction may still be extreme, but as they feel safely held, they are more able to bear this experience. It is during this phase of integration that the cycle is broken. Therefore, during adaptation, the child is resilient enough to their behaviour being challenged; indeed this is one important aspect of their lives in the wider society that they need to adapt to.

This description of therapeutic intervention highlights how the work is counter-intuitive. Adults can feel challenged by the child's expression of their mental anguish and emotional engulfment; their intuitive response can be to make threats, use punishments, and to feel and express anger. Undoubtedly, some children behave during these stages of the cycle in ways that need to be addressed, and this can be our intuitive response. However, such responses will not switch off the cycle, and are likely to intensify it, as they confirm the child's sense of self-loathing, worthlessness and failure. They need our support to face their turmoil, and importantly they need to know that they are still unconditionally valued. The time when they most need to send us away is when we most need to stay close. Similarly, when the child is feeling better, adults easily and intuitively provide comfort and closeness, perhaps not wishing to challenge for fear of triggering another episode of challenging behaviour. But this is the window of opportunity to challenge the child about their behaviour.

## REINTEGRATIVE SHAME

In the closeness of the primary relationship, the young child experiences attunement with the attachment figure. When growing independence results in the toddler doing something that the adult wishes them not to, in order to show an infant that behaviour is unacceptable, the caregiver breaks this closeness. This feeling of emotional separation from the attachment figure induces a feeling of shame within the child. This feeling inhibits the child's actions. If this is followed by sensitive availability, the child experiences relationship repair and return to attunement; once the child has stopped the undesired action, the attachment figure draws the compliant child back into the closeness of attunement. The child experiences relationship repair, and recognizes that they did something they should not. Over time shame allows the child to control their impulses; shame has modified behaviour. This is referred to as reintegrative shame.

If a child does not experience return to attunement, they are left with an unintegrated sense of shame. A toddler who is consistently left with this unintegrated sense of shame may develop shame-based identity. Shame does not inhibit their behaviour (as in healthy development) but becomes an all-consuming black hole into which the child falls. Cut adrift from reattunement, the child does not know how to repair the relationship. As the feeling of shame is not predicted to be replaced by that of attunement, there is little point in stopping an unwanted behaviour; the child has a feeling that there is nothing left to lose, and they are likely to go for broke. Lacking primary experiences of reintegrative shame, the child falls easily into a black hole of pervasive shame, with no hope of relationship repair or reattunement. This leaves the child with a stark choice. The anxious-avoidant child is vulnerable to despair, self-loathing and self-blame (leading to deliberate self-harm), whereas the anxious-ambivalent child, with nothing left to lose, is vulnerable to escaping this black hole by further acts of anger and violence.

Without sufficient experience of reintegrative shame, many children will escalate their anger cycle as a defence against the overwhelming feeling of shame; each shame-inducing outburst is defended against by another, more intense outburst, so that the child's threshold of anger related violence increases over time. The root of this, their poor primary experiences, is easily lost sight of, and the child is seen as angry, destructive and violent. The cure, adult punishment and coercion, is not seen as adding to the shame-based identity that is at the heart of the problem.

As an emotion, shame develops before guilt. If we feel we cannot be seen, we do not feel shame. Shame is born in the experience of being discovered doing something wrong, and compels us to hide.

## Guilt

Guilt develops out of the experience of reintegrative shame and is a healthy response to wrongdoing, which allows relationship repair because it triggers remorse. The feeling of guilt requires a more developed sense of the world of others. We do not need to be seen in our wrongdoings to feel guilt and can feel guilty about acts unknown to others. Our feelings of guilt are experienced in our conscience. Guilt requires empathy and the ability to take the perspective of another, and form a mental representation of how our action must feel to the other person. The internal system that allows us to do this is linked in some way to the attachment system. Threat-related activation of the attachment system (i.e. triggered by perceived threat, loss or harm) deactivates mentalizing by evoking intense arousal and overwhelming negative emotions. This is adaptive: when faced with a threat it is more adaptive to think about your own safety than to consider how this affects the other person. The inevitable result for children with insecure attachment is that their pervasive sense of insecurity reduces their ability to form mental representations of another person's experience, inhibiting the development of appropriate guilt.

## Toxic shame

Children who have been left alone, humiliated and shamed by their unacceptable behaviour will disconnect from these negative feelings, which are split off because they cannot be contained. They are not able to re-establish emotional bonds with others after shame-inducing experience. This results in toxic feelings of pervasive shame. Adults' response to the child's wrongdoings can encourage either toxic shame or guilt.

# SENSITIVE RESPONSIVENESS

The anxiously attached child has not fully integrated their thoughts and feelings. In order to promote reintegrative repair adults balance two dimensions of attunement in their interactions with children: feelings and thoughts. The child experiences that it is possible to integrate these dimensions, which can be thought of as intersecting to create four possible domains of response from adults.

Attachment grows from the sensitive responsiveness of the attachment figure. Sensitive responsiveness is expressed both affectively (as the attachment figure responds to the child's emotional communication) and cognitively (as the attachment figures shows contingency with the child's thoughts through shared intersubjectivity and mind-mindedness). Figure 3.3 illustrates these domains.

The domain child centred/attunement is shared at moments of harmony and closeness. The child experiences reintegrative shame if the adult moves from the domain child centred/attunement to the domain child centred/breaks attunement in response to the child's transgressions. The attitude of breaking attunement should not be maintained for too long; a minute for each developmental year is a good guide. The return to attunement may also need to be led by the adult, as the insecurely attached child is likely to lack the relationship repair skills necessary, and to be unaware (initially at least) that the possibility for reattunement exists. If the child does not have this opportunity, they are left with a consuming and pervasive sense of unintegrated shame. Adults are dragged into the domain child directive/breaks attunement if they subscribe to punitive ways of affecting change or dealing with challenging behaviours.

This model provides carers with a map of the relationship dynamics that are taking place during episodes of challenging behaviour from the child, and so allows them to maintain their equilibrium as authoritative adults.

By responding in appropriate domains, the adult provides the child with the missing experiences of reintegrative shame, and avoids both adding to the child's shame-based identity, and being a doormat. The adult also avoids being pulled into unhealthy roles such as feeling like a victim, trying to rescue the child, or feeling angry and persecuting them, as these actions fall in the other domains of behaviour that are not selected under this model.

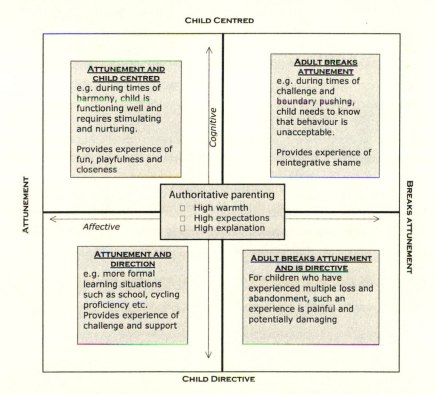

Figure 3.3: Domains of adult responses

## SQUEEZED PARENTING

Maintaining an authoritative role is not easy. Parenting is a transactional process, and the child is interactively constructing the parenting they receive. There is a complex interplay between our own inner tendencies and the child's coping mechanisms that disturbs our equilibrium and squeezes us in one or other direction on the continuum of parenting styles, pushing us off balance. The child pushes and pulls caregivers in a way that replicates the inconstant parenting of early disorganized attachment.

This can cause considerable difficulty in any parenting group. Adults with a tendency towards dismissive attachment cannot intuitively make sense of the changing responses in the adult who becomes more preoccupied-entangled, dismissing their over-concern as too liberal, lacking discipline, overly sympathetic, unprofessional, and being unable to understand why they fear the child's rejection. Adults with a tendency towards preoccupied-entangled attachment cannot make sense of the changing responses exhibited in the adult who becomes more dismissive, seeing their response as cold, punitive and over-controlling. These seemingly irreconcilable views can split apart caregiving teams (for example, a residential team, or a pair of foster carers) and can also split the wider support network, setting up conflicts between other adults involved in the child's life: birth parents, teachers, social worker etc.

It is as if the child, drowning in a swamp of early pain, is pulling on us to survive. The adult may turn their back and allow the child to drown, or they may feel they should jump into the swamp to rescue the child, although inevitably they will drown too. The authoritative parent is strong enough to allow the child to pull them towards their painful past, but by remaining secure within themselves, provide a way for the child to pull themselves out of the swamp.

So why do we get squeezed in this way? For some of us this may be habitual reaction when experiencing pressure or stress, but there is a deeper layer, which when understood points the way to surviving this pressure. The child's unresolved attachment history and heightened anxiety triggers threat responses in us. We feel anxious. Anxiety is there to keep us safe, but our security in our primary safety figure (which is the foundation of our attachment style) is threatened. Under this threat we are pushed towards compensating mechanisms that we have acquired at times of our own primary attachment experiences. The child needs us to consistently and predictably survive this pressure without losing our equanimity in order to begin to experience deep psychological and emotional safety within their relationship with us. Therefore two things need to happen. First, we need to be able to hold our own anxiety, so that our cognitions can kick in, because when they do we will have choices about how to respond and can keep the child's need at the centre of our actions; before cognitions kick in our anxiety is at the centre. Second, we need to be held by those around us: the organization, managers, colleagues, so that we do not feel overwhelmed by the task.

It is important to match the kind of individual support provided. Individuals who become dismissive need help in understanding the connection between the child's early trauma and their behaviour, but individuals who tend towards being preoccupied-entangled need education about the likelihood of feeling distressed by the child's rejection. The task is for each individual to be reflective enough of their own changing responses, by understanding the transactional nature of the developmental niche, through personal insight and the ability to be open to their own attachment experiences, so that they can monitor these tendencies and work hard to regain their equanimity. Adults will need support and guidance from trusted others: from colleagues, managers, the organization, and informal support networks.

## THE TRANSACTION WITH DISORGANIZED ATTACHMENT

From about age six, many children with a disorganized attachment begin to organize behaviourally. The attachment figure represents fear without safety, and the child struggles with this approach-avoidance dilemma by exerting control over, and punishing, the parent. In this transaction the parental figure is made to feel helpless and can respond by being hostile and helpless or hostile and fearful. Some parental figures respond by trying to exert themselves more, becoming intrusive and self-referential.

These feelings are a transactional response to the child's behavioural strategies. We need to be able to see them in ourselves and in our colleagues. Although understandable, these responses mirror the parenting styles that induce disorganized attachment in infancy. They are anti-therapeutic; they reinforce the child's IWM of fear without solution, preventing development of an organized representation of the caregiver as a secure base.

When we experience these powerful hostile and rejecting responses to the child's controlling-punitive behavioural organization we do not need feelings of guilt or blame, we need to recognize that we are responding to a powerful transactional pull exerted by the child, and should seek support from colleagues, support staff, managers, consultants and other trusted supporters.

## CONTROLLING OUR OWN AROUSAL

We need to be good at managing our own responses and emotional arousal. Expressions of fear are picked up in the amygdala (in the limbic area of the brain), which is sensitive to facial expressions and voice tone. When faced with challenging or disturbing behaviour, it is natural for our own arousal to increase. Such changes in arousal will be accompanied by changes in our behaviour, such as voice pitch, volume and speed of talking, body language and movement changes. These changes will increase the arousal level in the other person. As these changes will increase the arousal level in the other person it is essential that we are aware of our own feelings and reactions and that we become skilled at managing our arousal.

Learn and practise physical relaxation skills. Practise at times when you are not under pressure, for example, counting slowly to ten, slowing your breathing, clenching large muscles of the body (not hands, face, arms, etc.) and relaxing them. Recognize your own body language and movement changes when you become anxious, and practise controlling these. Although it can make us feel a little vulnerable, sharing these observations can be good team building. One useful exercise is for each person caring for a child to tell their colleagues, 'When I get anxious I...' The response of colleagues is critical. Non-judgemental support is required. If this is not possible, it is better to explore this in an exercise like this than during a difficult incident with a child. This exercise has three helpful effects. First, it allows us to look out for signs that others are coping less well today than the child needs; second, the power of these anxious feelings is significantly reduced when we verbalize them; third, we learn how to seek support.

## Substitute thinking

We may be thinking irrationally when we assume that things are done to us. In most cases, things happen, and they affect us. Recognizing unhelpful thoughts and replacing them with helpful ones requires practice. Another useful exercise, which can be used individually or in a group, is to identify some of the unhelpful, anxious thoughts that we have when faced with the child's extremes of behaviour (violence, collapse, self-harm, etc.) and then to try and reframe these thoughts in a more helpful way:

- 'It's personal against me' *or* 'It's not personal'.

- 'He's trying to upset me' *or* 'He has no idea how this makes me really feel, he's coping with his own feelings, and he's not coping very well'.

- 'He's doing this deliberately' *or* 'He's only trying to get his needs met'.

- 'It's hopeless, I can't cope' *or* 'I can only do the best I can'.

- 'Everyone is watching me to see if I mess up' *or* 'People are watching out for my safety. These are my colleagues and co-workers. I trust them and they trust me'.

## THE DRAMA TRIANGLE

In healthy development the black and white, either–or view of 'all-good' versus 'all-bad' caregiver disappears around age three. The thinking style becomes 'both–and'; ambivalence is possible; the caregiver is sometimes good and sometimes bad. Thinking is dialectic, that is; one view can be put up against an opposite view and integrated into a single new view. However, if this integration does not happen the child can be left endlessly recreating a dichotomous view of the world. The child becomes increasingly difficult to parent.

Caregivers can respond (without perhaps knowing) in ways that are shaped by the patterns of behaviour and coping that are a result of the child's early inadequate experiences and the adaptations they made in order to survive. When caregivers are functioning at this dichotomous level, they have different responses to the child, who is seen as either good or bad. Empathy disappears, and it is impossible to build consent, nobody can be truthful and no one trusts the others.

A useful model to equip adults to deal with this powerful pull towards unhealthy relationships is the drama triangle, described by Eric Berne (1964) in *Games People Play*. We can be pushed into unhealthy relationship roles by something inside us and by something inside the child. The pull can be powerful and hard to see, and arises when adults are unable to find the time to step back and think objectively. It can feel very natural and intuitive to respond in line with these roles, indeed, these roles dominate some people's behaviour in most situations. The roles have been learnt and internalized, often early in our lives. We can revert to them when under stress. We are drawn in by others acting complementary roles; we become enmeshed with the child and re-enact their relationship history.

The persecutor is the critical parent who says, 'It's all your fault'. They adopt a rigid, authoritative stance, and feel angry and annoyed with the victim, criticizing them, and wanting to punish and blame them, setting unnecessarily strict limits. They believe if you mess with them, you pay (retribution). The persecutor rejects the basic assumptions of the rescuer and the victim, and keeps the victim oppressed.

The rescuer is the doormat parent who says, 'Let me help you', and feels concerned enough for the victim that they take control, doing more than their fair share of the thinking and problem-solving. They rescue when they really do not want to, and yet feel guilty if they do not. They believe that the child is unable to solve their own problems and cannot help themselves. This keeps the child dependent, and gives permission to fail. They also expect to fail in rescue attempts.

The victim is the helpless-dejected parent who says, 'Poor me'. They believe that they are unable to solve their own problems, and feel victimized, oppressed, helpless, hopeless, powerless, ashamed, and hurt. Giving up personal accountability, and complaining about their powerlessness, they blame others. They believe that someone else should solve their problems, which are someone else's fault, and look for a rescuer who will perpetuate their negative feelings. The victim rejects the basic assumptions of the rescuer and the persecutor. If they stay in the victim role they will block themself from making decisions or solving problems, and will deny themselves pleasure and self-understanding.

If we think about the three models of parenting described above, we can see that the authoritarian model provides endless opportunities for powerful adults to act as persecutors, children to fall into victim roles, adults and children to rescue victims, and children to persecute others below them in the formal hierarchy or with less personal power.

The overly liberal/chaotic model provides opportunity for over-empowered pathological behaviours to persecute others who are unprotected by clear boundaries and expectations, for the persecuted to take on the role of victim and for well-meaning and well-intentioned adults and children to be rescuers.

The authoritative model, however, places appropriate authority with the parental role, respects rights and attaches responsibilities to these rights, providing clear expectations and explicit boundaries. It allows children appropriate autonomy, but does not ask them to be responsible beyond their developmental level. This is at the heart of the mutual and reciprocal relationship.

To get out of the persecutor role, ensure there is clear and explicit structure. Empower the victim, and do not take responsibility for their succeeding. To get out of the victim role, use and teach good problem-solving. To get out of the rescuer role use developmentally appropriate nurturing.

These dynamics can apply to any individual, group or organization that find themselves in dynamic conflict: managers, residential workers, children; or fostering agency, foster family, children; or school head, teachers, children; or senior manager, middle manager, workers; etc.

These roles can be understood as an expression of attachment insecurity. They emerge strongly when children are disorganized. The disorganized child has reasons for representing both the attachment figure and the self according to the three roles of the drama triangle. The attachment figure is represented negatively, as the cause of the ever-present fear without solution, attachment figure as persecutor with the child as victim, but also positively, as a rescuer. Although frightened by unresolved traumatic memories, the attachment figure may offer comfort to the child who then feels comforting availability and fear. With these two opposed representations of the attachment figure (persecutor and rescuer) meeting a vulnerable and helpless self (victim), the IWM of disorganized attachment conveys a negative representation of a powerful yet bad self (persecutor) meeting a helpless-hostile attachment figure self (victim). Sometimes the disorganized child may represent both their self and the attachment figure as helpless victims of a mysterious, invisible source of danger. Since the frightened attachment figure may be comforted by the tender feelings evoked by contact with the child, disorganized attachment may also convey the possibility of the child seeing their self as the powerful rescuer of a fragile attachment figure, reflecting the role-reversal that accompanies behavioural organization seen from about age six.

The insecurely attached child's coping strategies have a dramatic effect on the attachment styles of the other in a relationship. As the child squeezes the adult towards either a more dismissive or a more entangled insecurity, the adult can get caught up in a role that is derived directly from the change in their own security. Thus, the role that the adult is manoeuvred into in this drama triangle is a product of the child's coping mechanism and their own tendency to be squeezed towards being less secure under stress.

The first step in overcoming this is to recognize where our own insecurity is coming from (the child's poor adjustment) and to feel confident to seek support. The ability to seek support is a secure trait, not a sign of weakness.

It is quite possible for different adults to experience the same child's coping mechanism in different directions because the child's coping can push adults in either direction on the continuum, partly as a consequence of our individual tendency to be squeezed in one direction or the other, partly as a result of the way in which the child recreates the drama triangle roles already experienced in other, unhealthy relationships. As well as being confusing, and making it difficult for adults to come up with an adequate response to how the child is making them feel, this effect also triggers a dynamic between the adults that is best described as splitting.

In order to overcome the trap of the drama triangle, caregivers need to be able to do two further things: first, to disentangle their own relationship history from that of the child. It can be seductive to find ourselves in these roles if the role fulfils something in ourselves. It can also be difficult to resist if we are unsure what is expected of us. Thus the pull to rescue the child, or the need to discipline or punish, or the feeling of failure in the face of the child's resistance, can all lead us to remain caught in these roles. We need to be able to be objective about how the relationship is being played out, to step back from our entanglement in our own and the child's relationship history, and acknowledge that we have, perhaps unwittingly, found ourselves in the drama triangle.

Second, carers need to be able to conceptualize a healthy alternative. If we cannot imagine what a healthy relationship would look like in these circumstances, we are left with our intuitive pull into the drama triangle. Healthy relationships are mutual and reciprocal. Each party in the relationship endeavours to treat the other with respect and to show value. They are truthful (but don't use truth as a weapon to hurt the other), and are trustworthy, and willing to trust. They look to gain the other's consent. Communication is open and problems can be solved. We need to communicate messages of support not of rescue, victim, or persecutor.

We may need help. The drama triangle is not an overt set of behaviours, it is a hidden relationship bias that can be painful to acknowledge. It may be simpler for us to blame the child (persecutor), or else feel that there is nothing the child can do in their circumstances and we are uniquely placed to help (rescuer) or that there is nothing we can do, and we should just soak it up (victim). It is often the insight of someone outside the situation that can see the roles being played out, or it may be seen in reflective group discussions. Either way, adults working with these difficult relationship biases need support, guidance and time and space to reflect. The child has acquired habits and learned behaviours over a number of years, and for them to change will take time and the opportunity to learn new behaviours and ways of relating. In relating to the victim, persecutor or rescuer child ethically and honestly (as an authoritative adult) we achieve two things: the child has a secure base to explore, model and learn new relationship styles, challenging their negative self–other concepts and promoting cognitive re-evaluation, and we avoid being dragged into the drama triangle ourselves.

If the drama triangle is not skilfully contained, this unhealthy model of relationships contributes to the lack of integration in the child's inner world, reinforcing their lack of dialectic maturity (the ability to see shades of grey). At this point the adult needs to be able to give unconditionally to the child, without expecting any emotional repayment. It may be that all the child has to give back is their hostility. Adults should be explicit about their high expectations around behaviour, but should not expect the child to reciprocate emotionally; that may come later as the child begins to learn that we will value them unconditionally.

# PROMOTING POSITIVE AND REGULATED EXPERIENCES

All children need a balance between experiences that promote fun, playfulness and love (genuine warmth) and effective discipline. For the children we look after, this has usually been lacking in their lives up till now, and frequently, their challenging behaviour gets in the way; the ways in which they have learnt to have fun may be dangerous, frightening or anti-social, they may lack impulse control and be in a state of hyper-arousal (constant, deregulated stress); they are likely to have experienced overly restrictive discipline and punishment, or a lack of discipline and control, or both.

The following two lists are based on a handout given by Dan Hughes (www.danielhughes.org) at a presentation on caring for children with trauma-attachment problems.

## Strategies to promote the capacity for fun and love

Useful strategies include:

- being emotionally attuned to the child
- providing basic safety, security and food
- staying physically close
- integrating and resolving our own attachment issues
- using eye contact, smiles, touches, hugs, rocking, movement
- using positive surprises
- holding the child
- accepting the child's thoughts, feelings and behaviours
- reciprocal communication of thought and feeling
- giving opportunities to imitate carers
- having spontaneous discussions about the past and the future
- developing a mutual history.

## Strategies to promote effective discipline

These strategies include:

- making choices for the child, and structuring activities
- setting and maintaining the emotional tone

- providing natural consequences to behaviours
- being predictable in your attitude
- ensuring reattunement after shame-inducing experiences
- using getting permission, thinking, practising, having limits
- supervising the child in their activities
- showing effective anger occasionally, and avoiding habitual anger and annoyance
- being clear what is the child's problem, not yours
- using the child's anger to create a stronger connection
- limiting the child's ability to hurt you, physically and emotionally.

## BOUNDARIES, CONSEQUENCES AND SANCTIONS

Reasonable limits are not only necessary but are indeed welcomed by children who are reassured when they know the boundaries that adults are placing on their behaviour. If they know the limits, they can explore, knowing that if they go too far they will be told that they have, and the adults will have demonstrated that they care. Boundary pushing is part of natural development, and sometimes remembering that can help us not find it so challenging.

Children need firm boundaries and consistent behaviour management within a caring environment that approximates as closely as possible to a family environment, but the boundaries should address the needs of the children, not the convenience of the adults, and are better reinforced through rewards rather than sanctions. It is worth asking ourselves 'Do we need to make the child feel bad in order that they will behave well?' Applying sanctions under the misguided notion they will boost the child's motivation to learn to behave differently often leads to punitive strategies that worsen the situation.

Sanctions that work well for securely attached children (such as sending the child to their room) will increase the sense of mistrust, loss, rejection and abandonment that pervades the inner world of a poorly attached child. It is important that discipline does not reinforce these feelings. The message we need to give is, 'It is easier for you to be good and in control of yourself when you are close to me'. Sanctions that keep a child close to you, showing that you empathize with their difficulty, are more effective than the implicit message that 'nobody wants a naughty child'. Our actions have to actively demonstrate unconditional positive regard: 'No matter what you do, I want to be with you'.

Problem behaviours provide opportunity to express value towards the child and distinguish between the person and their behaviour. This is an opportunity for the child to experience that they are not all bad or all good. When a child who is insecurely attached becomes angry, this presents an opportunity to foster attachment. Attachment is triggered by perceived danger and terminated by perceived safety. Secure attachment grows from attachment behaviours eliciting sensitive responsiveness at times of emotional stress. Empathy for the child's hurt represents positive emotional engagement. How we behave when faced with challenging behaviour is a powerful reintegrative force.

It's OK to criticize a child's actions. Can we be sure we are doing it in a way that is not criticizing the child? Unacceptable behaviour is just that, unacceptable, but there are reasons why the children we work with cope in the way they do. It is not their fault that they cope like this; it is how they have learned to survive. However unacceptably they are behaving they do not need to be blamed. It is also important that the child is able to achieve any sanction given, so that they are not left with a sense of failure. Communicate sanctions empathetically: 'I know you felt angry, but when you hurt people, this is how you start to put it right'.

It is often suggested that children should pick their own sanctions or consequences. Adults who make this suggestion frequently note that the child is likely to pick something more severe than the adults would, perhaps making the point about the black hole of pervasive shame that the poorly attached child risks falling into. In general, such negotiation of sanctions is best if it is only rarely used, probably for times when the range of behaviour and sanction is far outside what is usual for the child. We all have to experience discipline. Leaving the choice of consequence to the child is giving up on discipline at the point when the consequences of unacceptable behaviour have to be faced. When it is appropriate to involve the child, it is essential that some time to reflect is also given: for the child to reflect on their behaviour and their choice, and for the adult to reflect on whether such a sanction is appropriate. This time for reflection allows you to continue to set the emotional tone.

There is, however, an excellent time for involving children in what sanctions should be used. When they are behaving well set aside time to collaborate with them in establishing agreements around rules, boundaries and sanctions. Then, when at a later time a sanction is given, the child knows that they were involved in, and had some choice over sanctions.

## Rules

As it can feel very oppressive to have to stick to lots of rules, it is helpful not to have too many. (Now's a good time to reflect on how we feel when we think there are too many rules governing our own life.) Rules provide opportunity for them to be broken and can be an endless source of unnecessary conflict:

- What are the house rules in your home?
- Why are they there?
- Would these rules make sense to a six-year-old?
- How do you ensure they are consistent and predictable?

## Logical consequences

Good consequences have a logical connection to the misbehaviour. If consequences are logical, children learn to accept responsibility for their mistakes and misbehaviour. For example, if a toddler rushes into the street, logic (and safety) dictates that they lose the right to play outside for a period of time. Then, when they are allowed to play outside again, the authoritative parents quickly encourages them to play within the rules. If an older child breaks a window, it is not logical for them to lose their favourite television programme, or go to bed early; but paying towards a new window is both logical and educational. When children are raised to accept the natural and logical consequences of behaviours, in time they begin to ask themselves, 'What will be the consequences of my making this decision? Am I willing to accept these consequences?'

In practice, particularly in the highly regulated environment of substitute care, this can be harder to do than it is to describe. However, adults can think carefully about consequences and make them as logical as possible. At least we can avoid illogical connections.

## POWER STRUGGLES

Poor impulse control, hyper-arousal, hyper-vigilance, witnessing domestic abuse, a sense of smallness and powerlessness can all make the child look for repeated power struggles. Behind this behaviour there is usually one of two dynamics:

- mistrust
- wanting to feel connected.

With mistrust the child wants to see how we will respond, whether we will abandon them. So we must not. We can walk away, but we should ensure that the child knows where we are going, and for how long. We could say something that avoids threats or decisions, 'I don't know what else to say for now, I'll come back later, when we've both had a chance to think about this'. And then we must do it.

The other dynamic is that the child wants attention, and to feel connected to another, but is only able to ask for it in a testing way. We should stick with them, providing the connection that they need. As they realize that we cannot be got rid of through these power struggles, the way opens for a better-adjusted relationship.

Caregivers need to be skilled at breaking the cycle of power struggles. These techniques are useful when you find yourself being dragged into one:

- Reflect to the child what is happening: 'Every time I ask you to do something, you say "no" or swear'.

- Tentatively acknowledge possible feelings behind actions: 'Sometimes young people who have been pushed around a lot feel more in control if they continue to refuse to do things they're asked. Is that what's going on here?'

- Acknowledge that it's hard for the child to get along with all the adults looking after them: 'I know it's difficult to have lots of people asking you to do things'.

- With warmth and humour, say, 'It seems to me we're in a power struggle. I ask you to do something, and you won't. If you were me in this situation, what would you do?' The child might be taken aback, or you might get an interesting response.

---

## Chapter Four

# Working for Recovery

## Relational Representation of the Secure Base

---

Children are complex social beings with extraordinary potential. Recovery from poor primary experinces is a personal journey that involves developing hope, a secure base, a sense of self, supportive relationships, empowerment, social inclusion, coping skills, and meaning.

## LEARNING OUTCOMES FOR THIS CHAPTER

Once you have studied this chapter you should be able to:

- explain and promote the concept of recovery
- provide secure base experiences
- understand the impact of early trauma
- provide vital parenting functions growing up in therapeutic relationships
- work with feelings and distorted thinking
- use unblocking techniques to overcome cognitive distortions
- employ empathy as a therapeutic approach
- provide unconditional positive regard
- understand the usefulness of saying 'no'
- match your individual approach to the child's attachment style.

## RECOVERY

Recovery means that the child is able to live a fulfilling life regardless of the problems and difficulties faced, that they come to experience earned security by acquiring a coherent account of their attachment experiences, and are more able to integrate their thinking with their feelings. Recovery happens in relationships. The human psyche is strongly inclined towards self-healing. Because attachment is indispensable to psychic well-being, rather than an obsessional focus on therapies, symptoms and cures, the quality of the therapeutic relationship is critical for success. Feeling safe and secure in a relationship allows for the exploration of problems and the discovery of methods for overcoming them. Once a secure base has been found, through the provision of a secure, reliable and consistent source of support and understanding, attachment behaviour is switched off and exploratory behaviour begins. The insecurely attached child can begin to revise their IWM and improve the quality of their other relationships.

Although the child is active, and to some degree competent in their own development, recovery begins in the minds of the caregivers. Exposure to warm, consistent and reliable caregiving can change a child's expectations of themselves and of adults. The ways in which the caregiver thinks and feels about a child's behaviours influence their way of caring and communicates to the child about their worthiness and effectiveness. Caregivers need to demonstrate, implicitly and explicitly to the child, that they are reliable, trustworthy, physically and emotionally available, and sensitively responsive to the child's real needs. The child's thinking and feeling is affected by this communication, and there will be a consequent impact on their behaviour and development, which over time creates a virtuous circle.

Recovery does not mean that the child's life somehow becomes as if early experiences of loss, separation, or trauma had not happened. Although poor primary experiences and unmet early needs adversely affect development, recovery is supported, not by seeing difficulties as weaknesses, but by focusing the child's strengths and abilities, considering carefully how to help the child live with or overcome their difficulties.

The child is at the point they are now, and recovery happens in relationships. We need to consider the child's protective strategies and coping mechanisms, which they have acquired to feel safe, and care for the child in ways that feel comfortable and acceptable to the child, and are not undermining, critical or threatening. Gradually the child can begin to mentally represent their new caregivers as protective and available and themselves as loved and lovable. The relationship becomes a secure base from which the child can explore the world, their past and the relatedness to others.

Recovery is not found in regression. Bowlby (1989) specifically rejected regression therapy. Work that is founded on attachment theory requires that we develop understanding with the child of their current difficulties, especially with interpersonal relations, and allow their relationship with us to become a secure base, building enough trust to be able to explore their current, wider relationships. It is important to recognize that the child's difficulties are rooted in real-life experiences, not fantasies, and to support exploration and review of earlier experiences to improve interpersonal relationships in the here and now. Emotional damage is frequently minimized because it is not easily visible. Without attachment the child has no place in the world, yet children have an amazing ability to spontaneously recover in the right environment, that is consistent, predictable, nurturing, and stimulating, with clear expectations and boundaries.

The path of recovery from trauma is likely to be different for each child. Recovery is often achieved in steps, or erratically. It can feel that progress has stopped, but it is often at such times that the child is consolidating their new experiences, and gathering themselves for later progress. For children who have suffered high levels of trauma, the recovery path may be one of getting worse before things get better. Beginning to confront the trauma means beginning to recollect memories that are often deeply defended against. This recollection is a painful process. The child can feel worse, and their behaviour is likely to reflect their mood. Progress is being made as they rework these recollections, but it can feel for the child (and those around them) that they are stuck. Once this reworking has taken place, recovery is much more likely to follow a steady or stepped path.

Child and caregivers are likely to be beset by doubts and fears, and therefore need to trust that the necessary support is in place. Change is in itself stressful, and often resisted. Recovery may stir up emotions that the child may have spent their lifetime avoiding or defending against, yet getting in touch with emotions is part of the process of recovery. And, although there will be gains from recovery, there will also be losses, which need to be resolved: for example, gaining the ability to trust others implies the loss of the distance from others that has made the child feel safe; taking control over their life may be accompanied by losing the role as the person who pleases everybody; recognizing that a parent was also an abuser, may be accompanied by losing them as a parent.

Recovering identity is a key indicator of recovery. Recovering identity can be thought of as the child or young person gaining the confidence and optimism that recovery can happen, increasing self-esteem, seeing themselves as a survivor, and becoming able to take appropriate responsibility for their actions and their own well-being, whilst rejecting negative identities based on being bad or unwell. Recovery also means that an individual is able to develop relationships that are supportive, understanding, consistent, reciprocal and based on trust.

Therapeutic work has a mystique around it that under-estimates the importance of work done by carers who have intimate knowledge of the child and opportunities for undivided time and space for the child to express anxieties, and to be listened to in an uncritical, sympathetic way. Recovery happens in relationships. It is within the intensity of close relationships that information about emotions is expressed and processed. The child achieves improved security, emotional intelligence and self-regulation in a relationship with a sensitive other whose own mental state is autonomous and secure.

There is no magical solution. We should be aware of the power of modelling; we are powerful models, and our attitudes, approaches and behaviours will be modelled and internalized by the child. In order to perform the task well parents, carers, educators and those that support them need to be adequately trained, to be clear about the task, and to feel valued. The child is unlikely to show appreciation, so this must be demonstrated by managers, peers and colleagues. The child benefits if the adults have a deep emotional pool on which to draw, which implies that they have dealt with their own attachment needs and experiences of separation and loss. If we are not taken up by our own attachment issues we are free to be sensitive to the child's communications.

## PROMOTING A SECURE BASE

Attachment embodies two contradictory drives: to be safe and to explore. The planned environment provides a symbolic representation of a secure base by structuring the child's environment as safe and sensitively responsive. With a secure base the child can begin the exploration of past and present relationships that begins the process of recovery. Recovery implies moving toward earned security and the interdependent autonomy of healthy adulthood, and recognizes that a therapeutic approach needs to replicate the characteristics of a secure environment for a child who deeply mistrusts being cared for, protected and benignly regulated.

The child's lack of stress regulation needs to be compensated for, to allow them to adapt to acquired developmental injuries, to learn how to regulate stress, and to learn to relate to others. A therapeutic approach looks for positive outcomes unique for each child. An essential element for promoting change is our own personal enthusiasm and hopefulness. As well as bringing creativity and playfulness, adults need to be available, but not too available. That is, sensitively available to the child, but mindful of their own needs and able to set and maintain boundaries. The anxiously attached child does not require adults who are doormats.

The child's general needs for food, warmth and shelter, safety, security and stability, physical contact and warmth, love and care, play, exploration, encouragement and risk, education, expectations and a purpose to life, all need to be met. Whilst healthy development for all children requires that these needs are met, insecurely attached children require further consideration of specific needs and strategies. The deficit of their primary experiences needs to be recovered. Due to unintegration of thoughts and feelings, children with anxious or disorganized attachment lack emotional intelligence, that is, awareness of and ability to manage their own emotions in a healthy and productive manner.

There are two broad categories of emotion: emotions that are easy to cope with and promote productive behaviour, and emotions that are extreme, difficult to manage and block productive behaviour. Unrealistic interpretations are the cause of many of the second class of emotion; a more realistic interpretation of events for the child can free them from the difficult emotion. Understanding the links between events, the interpretation of events and the emotions that follow is an important key to resolving emotional difficulties.

Parenting style, how much structure, nurture, time, attention, playfulness and challenge a parent or carer brings, is crucial. Authoritative parenting is warm, responsive, accepting, and empathic.

It is essential both to establish and maintain appropriate professional boundaries (workers are neither distant nor involved, but are engaged) and to establish and maintain a low-arousal environment, in which adults set and maintain the emotional tone, as this promotes trust in adult authority: adults are in charge and ensure safety.

Progress is likely to be slow, especially in the first year or two. The child will remain stuck in their familiar ways of coping and needs time to realize that carers can and do care for them. They need to become comfortable with the unfamiliar feelings of being dependent yet safe, exposed yet understood.

We will need to protect the child from activities and experiences that are upsetting or re-traumatizing, but should not be afraid to talk to the child about traumatic events the child brings up. Dialogue is therapy, although it is important that we proceed gently, and are ready to back off if the closeness of the moment or the psychological intimacy seem to frighten the child, as their fear will trigger aggression or withdrawal. The child needs to experience (perhaps for the first time) the constant and consistent presence of caring adults, and to feel that boundaries are imposed by adults to keep them safe, with the knowledge that they are valued.

Undertaking projects such as Life Story Work, to facilitate identity development and a sense of place and belongingness, helps a child to understand their own journey. For each of us, our sense of identity is embodied in a personal narrative that includes different versions of the self. Anxiously attached children have a problem-saturated personal narrative, which they have internalized as their primary self-description. Their problem stories and identities are created, lived and kept alive by their connection to important others, but are then frequently externalized in order to disconnect the problem from the child's inner self-description. In providing a new narrative, it is important to emphasize the positive exceptions to the problematic personal narrative. Writing (such as personal journals, and letters), Life Story Work, play, establishing relationships that can be trusted, and sharing experiences of conquering problems in groups can all amplify change. Becoming engaged in education and the wider community can offer meaning, purpose and a sense of belonging. Talking about problems, discussing issues, and acknowledging feelings are important to provide a secure base for the child to explore and develop a widening vocabulary of emotional language. Talking about feelings is far less destructive than acting them out because we are unable to talk about them, or suppressing/repressing them because they are overwhelming. The message for the child is that there is nothing so terrible it cannot be talked about.

## BEING 'REAL'

Human beings need fantasies in order to thrive and develop. However, vulnerable individuals can become confused between fantasy and reality in relationships and risk acting on the basis of a fantasy as if it were reality. This is especially so if individuals lack the capacity or support networks to express any worries and work through any confusion. Being 'real' challenges the child's distorted thinking. Distorted thinking relates to type of mood and triggers negative thoughts about the self.

The therapeutic task requires qualities and skills within the adult. The child needs to feel safe enough in their relationship with us to recognize and process their emotions, knowing that we can contain, handle, and help them to understand and regulate their arousal. As adults, we require realness; that is, that our feelings are available to us, we can acknowledge, explore and reflect on them, and we can communicate those feelings when appropriate. Being real means that we are prepared to gently, respectfully challenge the child's distorted thinking about themselves, their experiences and the world, whilst providing support in the face of troubling feelings and heightened anxiety. Integration of thought and feeling is encouraged in the space where the child's feelings are accepted as real and bearable, whilst their thinking is challenged.

Being real also requires that we are compassionate, honest and straightforward in our explanations. We need to be able to genuinely prize the child's feelings, opinions, and their person, so that the child can feel that we take pleasure and pride in them. We also need to be able to show acceptance, accepting the child as an individual person having worth in their own right, and find enjoyment in each other's company. We need to be able to use trust, and hold a genuine belief that the child is fundamentally trustworthy. And we need to use our curiosity: to really sense, hear, feel what life is like for the child, showing genuine interest, and exploring together. Crucially, as adults we need to be able to use and display our empathy, the capacity to imaginatively enter into the experiences of another human. Empathy requires emotional literacy, and therefore teaches it.

## TRAUMA AND THE INTERNAL WORKING MODEL

The child with attachment difficulties has developed an internal working model of themselves as worthless, and others as hostile and rejecting. This IWM has emotional and cognitive components and exists on the edge of consciousness. Traumatic events such as abuse and neglect, and fear-inducing parenting disorganize a child's attachment. Episodes of fear are layered in the child's thinking and reinforced through experience.

Fear is a natural response to danger, and allows the threat response to be triggered. As human beings, our response to threat is fight, flight or freeze. The amygdala plays an important role in the triggering of these reactions. Under threat, danger signals are communicated simultaneously via the thalamus to the amygdala and to the cortex. However, the route to the amygdala is faster, and it is already responding to danger by the time the signal has arrived in the thinking part of the brain, the cortex.

The amygdala produces automatic emotional and physical responses. The amygdala is unconscious, and emotional reactions can be formed without our having any consciousness of the stimulus, but cognitive responses are not so closely tied to our automatic responses. This means that once we have thoughts (cognitions) we have choice over our response.

However, attachment insecurity and disorganization impair impulse control, and so responses are often acted out before cognitions can catch up. Further, emotional memories in the amygdala appear to be permanent; there is survival value in never forgetting a threat. The amygdala does not make fine distinctions between stimuli, and it is biased towards fear responses to traumatic stimuli. Once a memory is stored, later exposure to similar stimuli trigger a fear reaction. So the fear and insecurity of poor attachment experiences, abuse and neglect permeate the child's IWM and feed the formation of further distorted self–other thoughts and feelings.

The traumatized child now has thoughts, feelings and behaviours that perpetuate the distorted self–other concept of the IWM, which are further elaborated and reinforced by their interactions with others and their life experiences. The child will acquire a set of self-fulfilling prophecies based on these distortions. Following the work of Young, Klosko and Weishaar (2003), it is possible to identify five components of these distortions.

- The child misperceives events so that the distorted self–other concept is reinforced. Information that confirms it is accentuated, but information that contradicts it is minimized or denied.

- The child blocks powerful feelings, preventing conscious awareness of distorted self–other thoughts and feelings.

- The child engages in self-defeating patterns of behaviour and relationships that trigger or reinforce distorted self–other concepts.

- They avoid relationships that challenge or contradict their negative self-belief.

- The child engages in relationships in such a way that they elicit negative responses in others, especially their caregiver, and so reinforces their self-belief in their worthlessness.

Recovery requires that we allow the child to diminish the intensity of the memories, emotions, bodily sensations and thoughts that accompany these trauma-induced self–other beliefs. Over time, living in a therapeutic environment and growing up in therapeutic relationships, the child can begin to form new emotional and cognitive linkages that allow their subjective experience of the self and others to alter. Good experiences of the self and others feed back to contradict the internal working model. Unresolved attachment issues become recoded in the context of a safe, less stressful developmental niche. Revisiting old trauma in a safe environment helps revise memories so that they become less distressing and more tolerable.

We need to resist their ability to avoid relationships that challenge their distorted self–other concept. Through re-parenting, the child can begin to acquire an internal representation of the other as responsive and available, as a source of safety, comfort and encouragement, and of their self as worthwhile and effective. This internal organization contradicts the IWM, developed from early attachment experiences, and promotes cognitive restructuring. The traumatic experiences are not removed, but the child's self–other belief changes.

## GROWING UP IN THERAPEUTIC RELATIONSHIPS

Usually, children come into the care system because of their behaviour, or the behaviour of those looking after them, or both. Behaviours come from and influence thoughts and feelings (our inner world). Traumatized and anxiously attached children often present behaviours that are disturbing, difficult to live with and destructive to themselves or to others (or both), and our work is often thought about in terms of changing these behaviours. This is not unreasonable, after all, behaviours can be seen and behavioural changes are an obvious way to measure change.

However, behaviours do not happen in a vacuum. Most behaviour depends on context, and understanding the context that behaviours occur in is important. Trauma and insecure attachment keeps the child caught in an unhealthy adjustment. When these behaviours, thoughts and feelings are unhelpful, dangerous or disturbing, our instincts are to help. Often, the child is locked into thoughts, feelings and behaviours that have become a self-fulfilling prophecy. Work that promotes recovery needs to break into the dynamic of the child's inner world at each part: thoughts, feelings and behaviours, influencing each component, which in turn influences the other components. Growing up in active, collaborative, therapeutic relationships challenges these self-supporting influences through new life experiences.

## RE-PARENTING FOR RECOVERY

Caregivers perform vital functions for recovery. They signal unconditional regard by looking past the child's behaviours to their unmet needs and feelings. They support recovery by caring for the child in the face of their hostility or over-dependence. They promote autonomy through education and correction, not punishment, as a response to misbehaviour. They build consent, encourage trust and develop the child's self-worth by showing their willingness to change ineffective strategies. They confirm the child's identity and sense of belonging through appreciation of the child's past. They encourage self-belief by their commitment to the long game.

### Fun and playfulness

It is more difficult for the child to be oppositional and negative when you are having fun together. Carry out activities in an upbeat atmosphere of warmth, empathy, spontaneity, optimism, cheerfulness, and fun. Learning occurs in an enjoyable environment in which the message is presented in a positive manner, with the emphasis on action. Choose activities that encourage success and self-enhancement, rather than self-defeating tendencies.

Fun and playfulness need to be managed taking into account the arousal level of the child, time of day, other challenges that will arise, etc. By managing the level of arousal (see Chapter 2), it is possible to contain the child's arousal engendered through playfulness so that the child is not hyper-aroused when faced with the next challenge. For example, insecurely attached children often find bedtimes difficult, as being left alone brings up older feelings of being abandoned. Knowing this, the authoritative parent reduces the child's arousal near bedtime through structure (a planned routine at bedtime) and soothing nurture (a warm, inviting and cosy bedroom).

## Mirroring

Mirroring involves active, empathic listening, and responding rather than explaining, fixing, and advising. Mirroring can help parents soothe and solve troubling situations by hearing and mirroring what their children are saying.

## Attunement and co-regulation

Attunement is a natural state of mother and infant, which has physiological characteristics (breathing, body language, facial expression, etc.) and is the process of matching emotions through play, acceptance, curiosity and empathy. Through this close attunement, the infant's caregiver enables the young child to develop the ability to regulate their experience of stress and distress, and to control their feelings and impulses. Attunement occurs when the parent is aware of their own feelings and sensations, and at the same time recognizes how the child is responding, and can communicate their awareness back to the child. This carer–infant dyad can be recreated with older children through:

- warm touch
- matching physical rhythms
- giving genuine praise
- describing shared experiences
- avoiding questions
- using child-centred language
- sitting at the same level as the child
- referring to common interests.

Co-regulation involves turn-taking and mutual action. It can be developed through simple turn-taking games, allowing or insisting that the child takes their turn, whilst, at the same time, the adult assertively takes theirs.

### Validation of the child's subjective experience

Affirmation, confirmation and recognition of the child's current experience, and communicating to the child that you can appreciate and understand how they are experiencing the world now, are all important aspects of re-parenting. This also involves communicating to the child that you can see, and understand why, they are angry, scared, anxious, etc., and not trying to get them to see the world from your point of view, reassure them, or get them to feel something different.

### Containment of feelings

Containment of feelings means being strong enough and kind enough to be able to stay with the child's overwhelming feelings without collapsing, perhaps by breaking down into tears, or saying you've had enough; or changing the subject, or trying to change the child's mood (deflecting); or retaliating, and attacking the child in some way to defend yourself and alleviate your sense of unfairness or powerlessness.

### Relationship maintenance

As adults working with the insecurely attached child, we need to carefully consider relationship maintenance. Relationship repair is moving on from damaging interactions, without pretending that they have not occurred. We should ask ourselves, 'What am I going to do to maintain my relationship with this child?' We cannot leave this relationship maintenance up to them; if they could do that they would not be poorly attached, and we would not be looking after them.

## WORKING WITH FEELINGS AND THOUGHTS

### Thinking relates to feelings

Certain thoughts tend to trigger specific moods, and certain moods encourage us to think particular thoughts. Being able to identify these links gives us a way in to the child's lived experience. A perceived threat provokes feelings of anxiety, whereas a perceived loss raises depressive thoughts. If we think that someone has done us harm, we tend to feel angry, but when we think we have done bad things to someone else, we feel guilty. For many of the children we look after, these feelings and thoughts do not occur alone, but come mixed together: perhaps despair over a lost parent, anger at their abuse, guilt from telling and anxiety in case they return. The child will need help unpicking their thoughts and connecting these thoughts to their feelings. Recognizing these connections can give us a way to help the child understand what they are experiencing. We need to go gently, being ready to back off in the face of their need to resist. We also need to be comfortable enough not to feel we need to reassure the child. When we say, 'It's OK', the child screams out (to themselves at least) 'It's not OK! Don't tell me it is!'

## Skewed thinking

A thought is not a fact. It is important that the young person has the opportunity to learn to recognize skewed thinking. Thoughts like 'I'm totally worthless' or 'Nobody likes me' are based on negative feelings rather than current experience. Thoughts, feelings, behaviours, memories and experiences interact on each other to produce our mind set. Clearly, it is helpful to ensure that the young person receives more positive experiences, but they also need to learn how to disentangle their negative feelings about themselves from facts. For the insecurely attached child, their internal working model ensures a template of skewed thinking through which they predict relationships based on the paucity of their primary experiences, seeing themselves as unwanted, unworthy and unlovable and others as hostile, rejecting and interfering. Common forms of skewed thinking are:

- jumping to conclusions, mind reading, assuming that other people are thinking bad things about them, without foundation

- fortune telling, making negative predictions about the future without knowing what the future holds, 'Nobody will miss me if I die'

- all-or-nothing thinking, thinking that they must please others all the time or they will not be liked or wanted, 'If I am not perfect, I am a total failure'

- over-generalization, when a single, negative event is seen as a never-ending cycle of defeat, making negative global statements and applying negative labels to themselves

- personalization, blaming themselves for things that are not their fault

- having a mental filter, dwelling on negative thoughts and filtering out the positive
- catastrophizing, over-estimating the chances of disaster
- asking unanswerable questions, such as 'Why am I so useless?' or 'Why do other people always get treated better than I do?', both of which are untrue and unanswerable.

# UNBLOCKING TECHNIQUES

It is not always enough just to recognize unhelpful thoughts when we experience them. They are often wrapped up in our automatic thinking and built on underlying beliefs and assumptions that come from our core beliefs. Various types of unhelpful thinking may require unblocking in different ways. Unblocking techniques can be used individually, but they are also effective if they are used in groups.

As well as being useful for unblocking our own unhelpful thinking, unblocking techniques can be used with the child to help them think about things in a less distorted way. If you are helping a young person with this, remember to remain tentative in your suggestions, not critical or judgemental, or too certain. Encourage the young person to ask three simple questions:

- What is the evidence for thinking like that?
- Can I think about this another way?
- Where is this kind of thinking getting me?

## Catastrophizing

Help the young person to explore possible outcomes in two columns, positive and negative. Order each column from the most positive to the least, and the least negative to the most. Subject each outcome in the negative column to the question, 'Would this be totally unbearable if this happened? If so, in what way?'

## Negative filtering

Suggest that the young person define what counts as a positive event and maintain a simple, two-column diary: date and positive event.

## Personalizing

Help the young person to construct a responsibility pie, by drawing a large circle and listing all the people and events that have contributed to a negative event, including themselves. They should then give a responsibility percentage score to each item on the list. Remember not to exceed 100 per cent. Now draw unequal portions on the pie that represent each responsibility score on the list. It is never all the child's responsibility. Ask, 'What can change?'

# EMPATHY

Empathy is the capacity to imaginatively enter into the experiences of another human being. It is accurate understanding of the other person's experience on a moment-by-moment basis, and requires that we listen carefully and in depth to what the other person is saying so that we can enter their world without confusing it for our own. Empathy provides the sensitive responsiveness required for secure base experiences. Empathy requires emotional literacy, and therefore teaches it.

Empathic communication can be thought of as a set of skills, which you can learn and apply. Although at first this may feel a little false and contrived, as long as your focus is on the content and feelings that are being expressed by the child, you will be communicating empathetically. One skill is in how we observe behaviour. We can look at another person's behaviour in times of difficulty in one of two ways. If we observe their actions, i.e. their large muscle movements, we attribute the cause of behaviours to qualities within them, their personality, temperament, mood, etc. However, if we look closely at their expressions (eyes, faces, gestures, body language) we are looking at their mental state, and we attribute the cause of their behaviour to be something in the situation they find themselves in. This is the point of view that distressed people have a strong tendency to themselves. In other words, we see the causes of their mental state from their point of view. This is therefore a key tool in creating empathy.

Another skill is to learn empathic listening, although this can be a painful experience as the child struggles to express their feelings. Empathic listening is a key skill in building trusting relationships. We may be empathic by nature (it is often one of the qualities that brings people into the work), but we can still improve empathic listening by knowing the technique and through practice. When a child is telling you about any event that raises strong feelings, listen carefully for feeling words so that you are able to identify their positive and negative emotion, and describe what they are feeling. This shows that you are listening. Summarize the child's main points back to them. You might use a form like this: 'You feel...(*name the feeling*) because... (*give the reason*)'.Use their feedback to correct your summary, if necessary. You will need to be tentative. You may hear conflicting emotions, in which case state both. Ask for clarity if what they are saying is confusing. Empathy can also be demonstrated through supportive comments that specifically link the '*I*' of the carer and the '*you*' of the child:

- *I* can see that being told off has been very difficult for *you* to cope with.

- *I* can sense how angry *you* have been feeling about things.

- *I* can understand that it must be frightening for *you* not to know what plans are being made for your future.

Briefly sharing your own experience can be a form of empathy, 'When I had an experience like that, I found it very frightening'. There is no need to add any more to this statement; the child will know that you understand their position, but if we elaborate, we are beginning to talk about our experiences and move the focus from the child to us.

## Empathic attunement

This means showing, through tone of voice, facial expression and body language, that you can really see and appreciate the emotions that the child is experiencing. It is shown in simple, non-judgemental statements to the distressed child (e.g. 'This is really difficult for you' and 'This has really upset you').

## Reflection

You can develop the skill of empathy by practising a technique called reflection. Reflection creates mutual understanding and strengthens and builds relationships.

### Nine steps of reflection

1. Listen carefully to what is being said.

2. Identify the child's emotion (positive or negative).

3. Find an appropriate way to describe the feeling, but be tentative.

4. Bear in mind that it is better to be too strong than too mild.

5. If there are conflicting emotions, state both.

6. If it is confusing, ask them to clarify.

7. Mentally summarize the child's main points.

8. State the summary in words they would agree with, but don't patronize or break your house rules about language. You can use a form of words like this: 'You feel… (*name feeling*), because… (*summary*)'. If you need to be more tentative you can say, 'I think you feel…'

9. Use their feedback to correct your summary.

## Some don'ts

Don't give false reassurances; you need to keep it real. Don't say things like, 'Everything will be OK''. Even though this may be true at a later stage you cannot promise anything at this point because you really do not know. Glib reassurances show that you are not accurately reflecting the content and feeling being expressed by the other person.

Don't fall into the sympathy trap. Sympathy is a reaction which one person evokes in another: 'Oh, you poor thing'. The effect of sympathy is usually to suppress feelings.

Don't talk about yourself. The child does not feel supported or understood if we say things like, 'You think you feel bad, well when I was ill…'

Don't try to change the subject, to cheer up the other person, or to distract them in any other way. The child will feel that you consider their feelings and experiences to be trivial or unimportant, something that can just be brushed away.

Don't judge other people's feelings. Don't say things like, 'You shouldn't feel like that' or 'There's no need to feel anxious'. These are their feelings, and they are allowed to feel any way that they do.

Don't ever say, 'I know exactly how you feel'. You do not, and cannot. It is more likely to make the other person feel angry as it shifts the focus back to you, and seems to play down the other person's feelings.

## Blocks to empathy

Our own needs and fears can prevent us from portraying empathy, and lead us into trying to be helpful, or wanting to see movement and change taking place in the person or their situation. Empathy is also blocked when we do not want the person to experience any pain, and we try to protect them from it. We may also be unable to demonstrate empathy if we are too concerned with wanting to be liked and/or needed.

## KEEPING COMMUNICATION OPEN

Carers need to be good at finding ways of keeping communication open with the child. This can be difficult; the child may well be shut down to communicating with others as a way of defending against their past experiences. The anxious-avoidant child will have an array of strategies to avoid communicating about their inner world; it is too painful, and they know it is. The anxious-resistant child will resist communication, often through violence and angry outbursts, but also through hyper-kinetic activity. One of the most powerful ways of keeping communication shut down is by raising adult anxieties, so that adults can feel it is better to avoid the real issue. Carers need to develop listening and talking skills, to be able to sensitively and supportively explore the child's real experience, and challenge their distorted thinking.

Anxiously attached and traumatized children often have difficulty communicating their distress. When faced with a crisis, one of the most important things we can do is to keep the line of communication open. This can require imagination and creativity, and always requires that we, as adults, hold onto our own feelings, often in the face of powerful resistance from the child; sometimes the child cuts us off by withdrawing; perhaps to bang about in their room, breaking their possessions and confirming their own sense of worthlessness, sometimes running away, sometimes projecting hostility and violence.

## UNCONDITIONAL POSITIVE REGARD

All humans need love, warmth and affection to thrive, but the circumstances of the work, including the need for safety and transparency, mean that it is unlikely to be professional carers who provide the love the child needs. Unconditional positive regard stands in place of the intimate love that parents can provide children. Unconditional positive regard means that the adult accepts the child unconditionally and non-judgementally. The child is free to explore all thoughts and feelings, positive or negative, without danger of rejection or condemnation. Crucially, the child is warmly regarded as much when they do no meet standards of behaviour as when they do.

Essential though this approach is, it is also important to acknowledge that the child may not be able to draw this distinction between themselves as people and their actions. This is, after all, a fairly complex way of looking at things which even adults will at times find difficult. There is no easy answer to this dilemma, and no workable alternative to trying.

## Acceptance

The caregiver shows the child that they are accepted unconditionally and valued for who they are for their difficulties as well as their strengths, but not everything they do. Avoid moralizing or being judgemental, and genuinely respect difference. Acceptance of the child even when behaviour is not acceptable actively demonstrates that uncontainable emotions can be contained. Through the caregiver's unconditional acceptance the child experiences themselves as worthy of receiving warmth and support, which promotes healthy self-esteem and a sense of self-worth. The child is unconditionally accepted for who they are.

## SAYING 'NO'

Consistently applied and explicit boundaries that are fair and meet the child's needs promote a sense of safety; the child feels free to explore within these boundaries, and intuitively understands that the secure base represented by the committed caregiver is there as a safe haven when exploration brings the child close to real or perceived danger. Children push against these boundaries as part of normal and healthy development. When children are troubled and disturbing, boundary pushing can be seen in a hugely negative light; it is as if every action is seen as a symptom of trauma. The child who explores against the boundaries will welcome limits. Sometimes it is enough just to say, 'Stop'. This is best said in a firm, but emotionally neutral, voice and may be accompanied by a hand gesture. The hand should be open, the fingers firm, straight and together. The hand starts at about shoulder height, angled at 45 degrees towards the child. As you say 'Stop', bring the hand fairly quickly to just above hip-height.

Another useful word is 'No'. Remember that what we should allow a child to do needs to change as the child develops towards autonomy, and we therefore need to adjust the use of the word 'No' as the child's skills and independence grow. It is important to distinguish between reasonable and unreasonable requests, and be prepared to choose your battles. Be fair and remember that the child needs varied experiences when deciding which requests are reasonable; if a child yearns to jump in puddles every day, perhaps they could be indulged occasionally. It is easier to remain consistent if you've been reasonable in the first place. It is important to be consistent about the use of the word 'No' for all ages. The child will feel unsafe, and is unlikely to comply, if one person is saying 'No' when the others would say 'Yes'. If the child has worked out that 'No' is changed by begging, then expect lots of begging.

If you feel that all you ever say is 'No', substitute this by providing a choice. For example if the child is asking to watch a film that is too old for them, instead of saying, 'No' you could respond with, 'We can watch a film. You can choose from X, Y and Z'.

Reinforce your values by saying 'No' calmly. If you become shrill you risk alienating the child. Saying 'No' one time, calmy, firmly and with conviction will become increasingly effective over time. We need to listen to the child and validate their feelings. We can open up the lines of communication by hearing the child's side of the argument, even when we know the answer will still be 'No'.

## MATCHING APPROACH TO ATTACHMENT STYLE

Attachment types produce differences in the way information is encoded and processed. The anxious-avoidant child and the dismissive adult are uncomfortable with the emotional and psychological content of interactions. They allow others to do their feeling for them. They have structures to contain feelings, but are emotionally bereft and cut off from any experience of feeling.

They will respond best to practice that is explicitly engaged in the psycho-emotional aspect of the relationship. Adult carers need to be sensitively attuned to the child's emotional tone, whilst carefully enabling the child to recognize and acknowledge the emotional content of their experiences. In its simplest form, this is explaining to the child that the unrecognized feeling is fear, or anger, or anxiety, or perhaps hungers. The helping adult will have to carefully explore the child's emotional landscape, and slowly provide a new narrative that takes account of the lost feelings.

Care needs to be taken to push only slowly against the child's avoidance. As soon as they have gone as far as they can bear, we should pull back. To not do so will trigger hostile and angry defences against our probing, but to remain sensitively attuned to the child's struggle promotes trust in us, and a growing sense of safety in the relationship.

The anxious-ambivalent child responds better to practice that promotes a systematic and problem-solving approach. They are overwhelmed by feelings and need others to contain them. They lack internal structure in the way they present and understand their self, which they experience as emotionally needy and deprived. Uncontained, it spews out over anyone who is in the way, and the child has difficulty in monitoring or controlling the effect of this overflow of feelings. They need opportunity for exhilarating activities, structure and a practical focus. They also need to begin to think about the effect of their feelings on others and education in problem-solving.

For children with disorganized attachment, the task is to establish order in the chaos of their thinking and feelings, to provide as much of a sense of safety and predictability as can be provided without being oppressive. They need to experience their attachment needs being met many times in a predictable way, so adults need to provide very high levels of predictable nurture before the child's attachment behaviours switch on; attachment needs are met without needing to be signalled. The child learns that needs are consistently and predictably met, and this experience begins to promotes organization. They begin to be able to predict how they need to be to get attachment needs met, and form an organized strategy to do so. Without attachment organization, their coping mechanisms are an unpredictable combination of the other types. We need to stay with the child's frightening experience, without being frightened ourselves, and without becoming frightening, until some organization begins to emerge.

## THE ANXIOUS CHILD

Children with insecure attachment can experience a level of anxiety that is not well connected to the situation they find themselves in. Their anxiety is often compounded by anticipatory anxiety that means they will work hard to avoid stressful situations. Reassurance does not work; to be told everything is OK, or will be OK, does not address the enormity of the task the child faces.

It is important that the child begins to accept the powerful feelings of panic and anxiety. These are tremendously distressing, but they are not dangerous. However bad it feels at the time, fear levels always come down. Support them to allow the anxiety to peak and recognize that they survive. Encourage them to see how their feelings go up and down. One useful strategy is to start a journal, recording what makes their anxiety go up and what makes it go down. They can rate their feelings on a scale 0–10, with their worst possible anxiety attack as 10. They can rate their feelings against this.

We need to empathize with their feelings of being cut off, alone and trapped, and to explain that these are states of thinking and not states of being. Thoughts are just thoughts, but the reality is different. No one is ever alone or trapped: there are people there to help. (It is useful to identify who these people are.) Let them know that they only have fear to fear. The clear message is that anxious people are good people suffering from a bad problem.

Find safe ways for the child to feel independent, so that they can become more confident in their own ability. Encourage the child to set themselves simple goals based on their current functioning at home, at school and in social settings. The goals should be something they would like to be able to do that is a little in advance of what they easily achieve now. Encourage them to practise behaviours that take small steps in a positive direction, and to learn some relaxation techniques.

## Chapter Five

# Working with Conflict

Human are social creatures, caring for their young and living together in groups. Essential competencies for groups to work are required: self-awareness, self-control, empathy, co-operation, and the art of listening and resolving conflict.

## LEARNING OUTCOMES FOR THIS CHAPTER

Once you have studied this chapter you should be able to:

- understand your own conflict style
- use defusion skills
- use conflict as an opportunity to foster attachment relationships
- link attachment and the child's approach to conflict
- resolve conflict safely by using this understanding
- employ effective listening as part of a range of communication skills
- understand retaliation and power struggles
- use assertiveness in a model of conflict resolution
- ensure recovery following conflict
- use problem-solving techniques.

## THE NATURE OF CONFLICT

Conflict and disagreement are a normal part of life, and are inevitably going to arise in caring for and educating other people's children. Pro-social behaviours, such as caring, helping, sharing, co-operation, and sympathy can be seen as a set of problem-solving strategies that are the opposite of aggression. Problem-solving strategies are often acquired early in life; if children learn pro-social skills well, they are less likely to learn aggressive problem-solving strategies.

The way we behave in conflict may seem part of our character and natural to us, but we learned our conflict strategies somewhere in our earlier development; we do whatever seems to come naturally, so that these strategies seem to us to function automatically. In fact we have a personal strategy that we have learned; and because it was learned, we can always change it by learning new and more effective ways of managing conflicts. Some people handle conflict well, but poorly attached children, those with few pro-social skills, and adults under stress, will often have problem conflict responses. There is no easy way to resolve conflict situations. The aim is to find ways to increase trust, decrease fear and make some level of co-operation possible.

## INDIVIDUAL DIFFERENCES IN CONFLICT STYLE

One useful way of thinking about how we react in interpersonal conflict is to consider how we have a personal 'conflict style' that is a function of the importance we place on two dimensions: personal needs or goals and relationships. Conflicts arise when our needs or wants (our personal goals) are in conflict with another person's needs or wants. Both may be valid, and may be as simple as an adult wanting a child to go to bed on time, and the child not wanting to be alone. We have also learned from experience that conflicts between people can affect how they feel about each other, and in some cases can damage their relationship.

Our personal conflict style emerges from how important these two dimensions are to us. If we place all our emphasis on our personal goal, we do so at the expense of the relationship. However, if we place all our emphasis on not damaging our relationship, we might need to give up our goal. Although our way of balancing goals and relationships depends greatly on the context of the conflict, we each tend towards a conflict style that somehow feels natural to us, and has probably been learnt fairly early in life and reinforced through countless conflicts.

Recognizing how these two dimensions pull on us can give us powerful insight into our behaviour at times of conflict, and help us develop better conflict resolution skills in ourselves and the children we are caring for.

Conflict style models based on the managerial grid developed by Blake and Mouton (1964) provide a useful framework for thinking about how our responses in these two dimensions reveal five conflict styles: Avoidance, Accommodation, Competition, Compromise, and Confronting.

## Avoidance

A strategy of avoidance means that the individual stays away from interpersonal conflict, withdrawing from anyone who may challenge them and anything likely to generate a disagreement, even though this means giving up on any personal goal and withdrawing from relationships. Conflict triggers feelings of loneliness and helplessness (goal cannot be met) and thoughts of hopelessness and abandonment (relationship cannot be preserved).

## Accommodation

A strategy of accommodation is driven by the need to be accepted and liked by others, and so conflicts are avoided in favour of harmony. Relationships are valued and have to be kept smooth and unruffled, but personal goals are given up as unimportant. Accommodation arises from a belief that you cannot discuss conflicts without damaging relationships and fear that continuing conflict will ruin the relationship. There is a powerful urge to please the other person to avoid abandonment.

## Competition

A strategy of competition means that the individual's goals are more important than any relationship, which leads to a lack of concern for the other person's needs and goals. They assume that conflicts are either won or lost and they want to be the winner, and try to force the other person to accept their solutions. Conflict triggers feelings of winning at all costs and thoughts that other people's esteem and acceptance is unimportant. Winning can provide feelings of being powerful, but losing gives rise to a sense of weakness, inadequacy and failure.

## Compromise

A strategy of compromise comes from being concerned with both goals and relationships: looking for the middle ground and seeking a solution in which both sides gain something. Compromise means giving up part of your goal and persuading the other person to give up part of theirs in order to find agreements that work for both parties, and does not leave unresolved feelings. Compromise works well if both parties are prepared to compromise, but is less effective with other styles.

## Confronting

A strategy of confronting is perhaps the most effective, professionally at least. As well as wishing to resolve any negative feelings, conflicts are seen more as problems to be solved. The kind of solution that is sought protects each person's needs and legitimate goals. Conflicts can become a way of improving relationships by reducing tensions between people. Relationships are maintained by solutions that satisfy everybody. Although quite challenging, this is basically a collaborative approach built on being truthful that increases trust.

Obviously, when conflicts arise, each individual may be using different conflict strategies. Some individuals will move from one style that isn't working to another that might.

## INCONSISTENCIES IN CONFLICT STYLE

Although individuals often have a prominent conflict style, how we choose to react in conflicts is also to some degree influenced by the environment at the time. A competitive individual may choose to be avoidant when faced with someone more powerful, and an avoidant individual may occasionally stand up for their goals. We are also influenced by factors such as our professional role; many childcare professionals may, understandably, be less skilled at dealing with conflict at home than they have to be at work. Doing conflict well can be hard work, and it's natural that we cannot always sustain it. It is also helpful to think about how our inner security is squeezed by the traumatized child's coping mechanisms. As we have already seen, we each have a tendency to be squeezed towards being dismissive or preoccupied and fearful of losing the relationship. Under pressure we are likely to move in one direction or the other, tending to adopt a competitive or an accommodating style.

This squeeze is even more powerful when the child has a disorganized attachment. Adults can become overwhelmed by a child's chaotic inner world, and a behavioural coping style that is punitive and controlling. Caregivers can feel helpless and hostile, vacillating between punishment and despair. As well as contributing to placement breakdown, this reflection to the child of their chaotic inner world further degrades their ability to sustain an organized internal representation of the caregiver, hardening their disorganized attachment, and reinforcing their approach-avoidance dilemma.

If we see being good at conflict as a set of skills we can learn, and be supported to use, and we are able to be reflective about what we have done well and what we have done less well when we find ourselves in conflict, we can begin to practise in a more insightful, less intuitive way. It takes time, but we can learn to master our impulse to act in one way or the other way faced with conflict and become better at maintaining ourselves as secure adults who value relationships and understand the importance of protecting our legitimate goals.

## Sex differences in emotions and behaviour

The cerebellum (the top layer of the brain) is divided into left and right cerebral hemispheres. Crosswise fibres running between them are used to exchange information between the two hemispheres. These connections between the hemispheres, the most significant of which are the corpus callosum and the anterior commissure, are somewhat different in men and women. The area of the anterior commissure and the back part of the corpus callosum seem to be larger in women. The larger area of the commissure results in better communication between hemispheres, possibly accounting for some of the difference in the way men's and women's brains work; the female brain has more connections between hemispheres than the male brain. This means, for example, that women can often hold several conversations at once, and are more able to listen and speak at the same time. Men focus their attention more easily, cutting out distractions.

When emotional, the female brain is wired for speech, but the male brain is wired for action. This results in different responses to strong emotions: women may want to talk about their feelings, whereas men are more likely to want to walk away (the better option) or hit out. Although each sex can become frustrated with such different responses from the other, understanding that this is biologically driven can help us be more accepting of these different responses.

## CHOICES IN CONFLICT

When faced with conflict there are a number of ways we might react. The strategy we choose is often decided by context and personal conflict style.

### Prevention

Prevention can be useful. However resilient an individual is, we all have our breaking point; prevention of unnecessary conflict, in contrast to avoiding necessary conflict, protects us from becoming overloaded. It is particularly important during stabilization. Early in placement a child may seek conflict to alleviate the unfamiliar harmony of a low-arousal environment. If conflict is familiar it can be easier to understand than more co-operative approaches. It is necessary to survive this for long enough for the child to adjust in order that the work of reintegration can begin.

Adults should promote a culture of collaboration and co-operation: problems are there to be solved. Conflict can be prevented through clear expectations and by ensuring that rules and boundaries are explicitly stated, make sense to the child, and are not excessive. Genuine warmth should always be maintained, but we need to be aware that it also requires toughness. We may have to make difficult decisions because they are truly in the best interest of the child. Unmet needs are often triggers to conflict. If adults anticipate and meet the need, the child does not need to resort to conflict-laden strategies in order to have these needs met. Preventing conflict involves being aware of the child's needs, respecting their limitations and supporting them by creating an environment that doesn't push them past their limits.

Unnecessary conflicts can be reduced by carefully thinking about what it is that the child is doing. Is their behaviour disruptive, to whom and in what way? How do these behaviours make us feel, and what do we think about feeling this way? We should understand why we feel this way, and consider how we can hold those feelings. The child's behaviour may well trigger angry and hostile feelings in us. It is important to recognize that it's OK to feel angry and frustrated, these are genuine feelings at the time, but we also have to monitor and regulate how we may behave when we feel like this. We all feel confident, mentally alert and in control if we are physically stable and have plenty of oxygen in our lungs; adopt an upright posture, with both feet firmly on the ground and breathe deeply.

By preventing unnecessary conflict we reduce the daily experience of failure, break a culture of aggression that surrounds many disturbing children, improve the general quality of life for children and adults, and ensure safety. However, prevention may not allow the resolution of underlying conflict.

## Avoidance

Avoidance is not the same as prevention, and is a risky approach to conflict. Avoidance may be expedient, and sometimes is the only option, but it masks or ignores conflict, and does not address underlying issues. It is often driven by concerns about how a conflict will escalate.

## Defusion

Defusion of conflict is an essential skill. Skilful defusion allows a culture of safety to develop, and gives clear signals that emotions do not need to be thrown out into other people's lives in order to be lived with. Defusion can also buy time, allow tempers to subside, and allow other issues to be dealt with.

In order to defuse conflicts it is helpful to look for early warning signs as early intervention works best. We need to manage our own fear about where this is going, as our own anxiety will tend to feed the child's feeling of being under threat. It is essential to try and keep communication open. Relax and provide non-threatening physical proximity, and maintain unconditional positive regard.

Defusion through distracting or diverting can work well for young children, but older children may like a problem-solving approach. For this they will need to have confidence in you and feel that they can trust you not to be a threat.

A key skill in defusion is to listen well, and to empathize. If communication is open it may be possible to discuss and negotiate. Humour can be successful, but only works if you have a good relationship with the child where humour is already a familiar and welcome currency; otherwise it is a risky strategy as the child may feel they are being ridiculed.

## Confronting

Ultimately, most conflicts need to be confronted. The choice is how. Individuals who use a variety of violent responses may gain their goal in the conflict, but will damage relationships. Except for the use of legitimate power, violence is unethical and violent strategies are unethical and frequently illegal. Children that have come from backgrounds where violence has been used will have learnt violent conflict strategies. Adults need to guard against unwitting use of violence, for example, psychological violence or the misuse of authority (punishment used to resolve conflict). Children can learn to be skilful in confronting conflict through modelling adults who handle conflict well.

# OPPORTUNITY

When a child who is insecurely attached becomes angry in response to the consequences of his behaviour, an opportunity to foster attachment is presented. Attachment is triggered by perceived danger and terminated by perceived safety. Secure attachment grows from attachment behaviours bringing about sensitive responsiveness in the attachment object at times of emotional stress. Empathy for the child's anger represents positive emotional engagement. If we can hold our own and the child's emotions, the child feels that they themselves are held emotionally. Attachment security is promoted when the child feels held physically and emotionally.

It is healthy for children to experience that relationships go up and down. Conflict resolution provides an opportunity for the child to learn that conflict doesn't have to destroy a relationship, and provides an opportunity for you to express value towards the child, distinguishing between the person and their behaviour (unconditional positive regard). Within a therapeutic relationship, this can provide a secure base for the child to explore being neither 'all bad' nor 'all good'.

# ATTACHMENT PATTERNS AND CONFLICT STYLE

The child's pattern of attachment influences their conflict style. By thinking about the child's attachment style, adults can provide important opportunities for the child to develop their conflict skills. In working effectively with conflict the long-term task is to help the young person develop a healthier and more effective response to conflict. To develop pro-social conflict skills for children with an anxious-ambivalent attachment, the task is to help them develop empathy by communicating how their actions to meet their goals make others feel, and to develop the ability to recognize and understand that others also have rights and feelings.

Anxious-avoidant children need help to be more confident and assertive, to recognize that they too have rights and their feelings and wishes carry weight. When in conflict with others they need clear messages that their legitimate goals can be met without scarifying the relationship; adults will need to push them to expect that their legitimate goals can be met.

Children with disorganized attachment need help to become more courageous and to feel less powerful. Disorganized attachment induces an IWM of the self as powerful yet bad, and the attachment as hostile and frightening. They may have developed controlling-punitive behaviours to cope. As well as needing courage to face the fear inherent in their relationship with their attachment figure, our ability to withstand their controlling behaviours will reduce their sense of being powerful yet bad. We may need to manage controlling behavioural organization, which can overlie their disorganized mental representation of their primary attachment figure. These children require a high degree of structure and clear and consistent responses to unwanted behaviour, always underpinned by unconditional positive regard. They may need a great deal of containment during conflict which they will find to be frightening, highly unpredictable and unlikely to have a good outcome. In handling this, adults should ensure that the child's legitimate goals are met in some way, and that meeting them is distinguished from the child's own wild strategy. For example, the conversation after a conflict over bedtimes might be something like this: 'It's perfectly reasonable to stay up later at the weekend, but that doesn't mean you can go to bed late every night. If you want to stay up this weekend, you need to help me straighten up this mess'.

The hope is for the child to develop more healthy approaches to managing conflict. With guidance and good role models, anxiously attached children can learn to compromise in conflicts and become more adept at collaboration.

## KEEPING YOURSELF SAFE

Be sure that you respond to genuine concerns for safety in a predictable and consistent way, but do not use concerns for safety as justification to escalate the situation. Often danger can be avoided, but remember that the usual exit from danger would be through a door! It might be necessary to call for physical help. If entering a volatile situation it is sensible to:

- inform colleagues what you are about to do
- keep the door open, and do not allow a volatile individual to get between you and the door
- do not increase the temperature of the situation by your own approach
- think about the hidden messages you are conveying through body language, facial expression, and tone of voice
- be unobtrusively watchful for danger.

## COMMUNICATION: 'THERE ARE TWO PEOPLE IN THIS'

It is important to recognize what the other person is doing to defuse or de-escalate the situation. The child will have some skills (behaviours) in conflict resolution and needs to practise them. For a variety of reasons these behaviours may not be the same as ours, but that doesn't mean they don't work. It is important not to see everything they do as adding to the problem. For example, the child may swear at you and walk away. Whilst this is not acceptable behaviour, it may be their way of taking some responsibility to resolve the conflict or calm down. We can acknowledge this, and even reward the positive nature of the behaviour. (For example, part of the conversation that follows the conflict might be something like, 'It upsets me when you swear at me, but I think you did a good thing when you walked away to calm down…')

### Behaviour is a language

At times, when we are being abused, intimated or hurt by a child, we may feel completely justified in making judgements about the child's behaviour, and may have every reason to feel as we do about the way we are being treated. However, the time of the conflict is not the time to reconcile these feelings. We're the adult and can sort that out later. Not all behaviour is rational and intentional. The way someone behaves is tied up with their thinking and their feeling, and there is little point in becoming angry. It is better to ask yourself: 'What does this behaviour mean?' The way we act now provides a role model for the child in future conflicts. We can resolve the conflict more effectively, and do less damage to the relationship, if we manage these feelings. The child probably feels as justified in their feelings as we do.

## Communication

When dealing with conflict it is important to be aware of how what we are communicating is likely to affect the child. Adults have a great deal of power in these situations, and children will therefore want to defend themselves and equalize this. Adults think and communicate with words. Children think symbolically. We are the skilled communicators and can easily use our expertise and power to our advantage. We may habitually meet conflict with conflict, or be concerned to win. The child's worldview is influenced by an IWM that predicts rejection and hostility, and provides expectations founded on a sense of worthlessness.

As conflict escalates you can be certain that communication is not happening effectively. Communication uses cognitive capacities, which are easily overwhelmed by the emotional content of the experience. We say we want to help, but can sometimes use communication forms that are unhelpful, such as using criticism, labelling, diagnosing, giving orders, making threats, moralizing, questioning, giving advice and diverting.

Conflict is stressful, and stress triggers a flight/fight response, releasing powerful chemicals (hormones). Poorly attached children, in a state of hyper-arousal are disproportionately flooded with these hormones. Commands to 'Calm down', 'Make right choices', 'Think of the consequences' and telling the child off are always stressful (more hormones) and may feel more like threats than attempts to resolve the conflict. This is also very stressful for us. We may have competing demands to fulfil. Unless we have a plan and a clear model to work to, we are likely to be disorientated, thrown off balance and unsure of the most effective strategy.

## EFFECTIVE LISTENING

An angry, upset child, programmed for conflict, wants and needs to be listened to. We need to let the child know that we are on their side, that we want to help, but in a way that lets them know that we are not going to collude with unacceptable behaviour.

- Stand in his shoes.
- What does it feel like?
- Now listen…

Hold on to your own emotions, and then deal with the other person's emotions before any other issues. If you deal with their feelings, it is difficult for them to continue to target their aggression onto you.

## Listening skills

### Step 1

- Be aware of personal space; standing too close is threatening.
- Adopt body language that says you're involved and shows you're listening and genuinely interested.
- Be aware of your voice and control the tone, pace and volume.

### Step 2

- Encourage the other person to talk by using simple, non-judgemental statements ('You seem pretty upset').
- Ask a very few open questions, but do not interrogate.
- Use attentive silence, which can include head nods and therapeutic grunts.
- Be prepared with door openers and help scripts: simple statements that show empathy and concern and may offer a choice of action, but avoid telling the child to make choices:
  - 'You don't seem to be yourself at present.'
  - 'This has really upset you.'
  - 'I'm here to help.'
  - 'You could tell me what's troubling you.'

### Step 3

- Check out that you have understood and show that you have been listening carefully by paraphrasing what they have said to you. Let them know what you're doing and why ('I just want to paraphrase what I think you've said, to make sure I've understood'). Keep this brief, you are trying to listen to them, you are not using them to listen to you.

- Reflect feelings; listen out for feeling words and use these words when you describe how you think they are feeling. Be tentative: '(I think) you're feeling (*their feeling word; angry, fed up, etc.*) because (*paraphrase their main reason*)', e.g. 'You're feeling angry because your mum didn't turn up'.

These reflective responses introduce a break in the flight/fight response. By continuing to use these responses, you allow time for stress hormones to dissipate, which is calming down. It can be hard to think clearly when faced with an angry child. It is useful to have some prepared scripts: in response to, 'I don't ****ing care...' you could say, 'I'll have to care enough for both of us'.

## KNOWING OURSELVES: WHY DO ADULTS RETALIATE?

Caregivers can be pulled into a form of retaliation, not from personal inadequacies, or a lack of self-control, or something that derives from our early childhood experiences, but from the same instinct to protect ourselves that triggers the child's aggression: a biological response that guaranteed that primitive humans could survive. We are hard-wired to respond to threat, and our retaliation can be hard to overcome. Long (1995) suggests that adults retaliate in a number of scenarios.

We can react to being caught in the child's conflict cycle. Although we do not start the conflict, we feel threatened and overwhelmed, and respond in ways that escalate the conflict. If we cannot own our retaliatory feelings, they will mirror the child's behaviour. Instead of assuming that the child doesn't want to co-operate, assume that they *do* want to, but are unavailable to do so, through no fault of their own. We need to think carefully, 'It's OK to feel angry and frustrated, these are my feelings at the time. That does not give me permission to retaliate'.

Children's attitudes and actions can challenge our strongly held views and core beliefs about how children should behave. This triggers strong emotions, our identity feels threatened, and we respond with aggression. The solution begins with our self-awareness, not with the child's behaviour.

We may retaliate because we have not used our usual skills and strategies, and become defensive and angry, 'It's all their fault! If they had behaved properly, I wouldn't have all these problems'.

We are not robots, and we are subject to the same developmental, psychological, and physical stresses as all adults. When we are in a bad mood, usually competent, dedicated, and supportive caregivers may not be able to cope with the child's behaviour, leaving us vulnerable to retaliating. We need to be good at recognizing our mood and lifting it. If this is habitual, we need help to understand where the mood comes from.

Sometimes, we may simply retaliate because we are worn out and can no longer manage not to. This is a good time to get someone else to take over. Remember: we don't have to win; we do need to find a solution.

Caregivers who are committed to helping a troubled child recover may develop a special relationship: the child enjoys and responds positively to our involvement, and the relationship seems to be mutually satisfying and rewarding. Over time this relationship begins to deteriorate. The child becomes demanding and mistrustful; we can feel bewildered and rejected. However, without the internal structures to feel secure in a relationship, the child fears this growing closeness. The child is not rejecting the relationship, but fears intimacy and rejection. While they are wrestling with this, the drama centres on us, and we feel angry and exploited, and rejected by the child.

Adult retaliatory behaviour has no therapeutic purpose. It destroys trust and degrades the effectiveness of the work. It succeeds in reinforcing the child's self–other beliefs that they are worthless and adults are hostile, rejecting and punitive. Our ongoing professional struggle is to become more aware of how the underlying reasons for retaliation affect us personally.

## EFFECTIVE CONFLICT RESOLUTION

It can be helpful to spend some time thinking about a child's learned conflict style (see Table 5.1). As well as identifying difficulties, try to think of any conflict resolution strengths that they already possess. One you have had an opportunity to think deeply about the child's conflict style, ask the child a parallel set of questions. This will develop insight into how they perceive conflict, and ensure that getting better at conflict is a collaborative process.

**Table 5.1: Child's conflict style**

| Adult thinking about the child | The child's view |
| --- | --- |
| With reference to the individual conflict styles model, what do you see their style to be? | What do you think most about when you have an argument with someone you like: being friends, or the thing you are arguing about? |
| How have they learnt this? Think about the child's history: early family experiences, experiences of being looked after by other adults, peers, etc. | What do your friends do when they have arguments? Do you think that's a good way to handle things? |
| How well does it work for them? | Are you happy with the way things turn out when you disagree with other people? |
| How well does it work for others? | How do you think it is for the person you fall out with? |
| Does it make them feel safe, or out of control? | What do you feel when this is happening? |
| Do they have insight into their conflict style? | What do you think you do when you fall out with someone? |
| What reinforces their conflict style in their current environment. | Is there something you would like us to do differently when we fall out? |
| What opportunity do they have to learn new strategies? | Would you like to learn other ways of handling things when you fall out with other people? |

When in a conflict, avoid becoming adversarial or defensive. See conflicts as an opportunity to engage with the other person; the initial task is to have an attitude where you want yourself and the other person to benefit from a shared decision (this is sometimes called win/win). To do this we need to find out what each person's needs are. In communicating your own needs, be assertive, and use 'I' messages, not 'you' messages. Do not antagonize the situation by defending yourself first. Deal explicitly with the child's emotions, acknowledging how angry they are. You do not need to agree with them, but you do need to show you understand their perspective. Keep committed to addressing the issue, not the person.

Once individual needs have been expressed, you can enter into negotiation. You may need to break problems down into smaller pieces, and it is worth trying to get agreement to look at one piece at a time. Keep focused on the issue and look for and acknowledge areas of agreement. Manage your own emotional arousal, and do not react to the child's rising anger, carefully challenging jibes, taunts and insults without getting angry, perhaps by saying, in an emotionally level tone, something like this, 'It's interesting that you say that, but I'd like to talk about what's upsetting you'. Make a trial proposal, perhaps suggesting a trade: 'I will do "A" if you will do "B"'. Offer to make an agreement time limited: 'Let's try this now, if it doesn't work, we can see if we can find another solution'.

Sometimes you will need help. This should not be seen as a failure on your part, but as an additional offer of help: 'We're not making much progress, I wonder if we spoke to X if they would have any ideas'. Agreement to involve another person is in itself a reduction of conflict, but they need also to be explicit about finding a win/win solution. They will need to gain a clear sense of the issues, but should avoid making suggestions, which they should elicit from the others.

When (or if) a resolution is reached, be clear about the agreement. Recap so that both of you understand, and do not have different opinions about what has been agreed.

## ASSERTIVENESS SKILLS

Aggression and submission can be understood as behaviours along a scale. Aggression can be seen as an attempt to get what an individual wants at the expense of another ('I win, you lose'). Aggression includes standing up for rights in such a way that the rights of others are violated in the process, and being self-enhancing at the expense of putting down or humiliating others.

Submission can be seen as the individual giving up what they want for the other person. Submission includes an individual having difficulty standing up for themself, voluntarily relinquishing responsibility for themself and inviting persecution by assuming the role of victim or martyr.

Behaviours along this scale are natural and universal, and are by no means wrong. However, they are often ineffective, especially in dealing with anger, aggression and conflict. On the other hand, assertiveness, which can be seen as a set of skills that can be learnt and need to be practised, can be highly effective at dealing with another person's aggression.

Assertive conflict strategies are best understood as a set of skills that are either switched on or switched off (you can be a little aggressive, but you cannot be a little assertive). Assertiveness can be summarized as 'I'm going to win some and I want you to win some too'. It is an individual expressing their needs, preferences and feelings in a manner that is neither threatening nor punishing to others and without undue fear or anxiety: standing up for their rights in such a way that they do not violate the other person's rights, and communicating honestly and directly with other people in such a way that assumes they are able to interact equally and take responsibility for themselves.

Assertiveness is shown in our body language (including posture, gesture and action), facial expressions, and vocal clues. We should ask ourselves, what would my voice say if the other person doesn't listen to the words, but only listens to the tone? It is important that we are confident that our abilities will ultimately work if we let them, but we may need to recondition and practise new reactions to aggression.

## Commonly used assertiveness skills

Being assertive does not come naturally; it requires a range of skills. Ensure that the feelings you are experiencing are expressed in the words you use, the way that you say them, and your body language. Sometimes, in difficult circumstances we may need to soften assertiveness. We can do so by speaking passively but presenting assertive body language, or the other way round. Use different voice tones. You may need to raise your voice to get attention, but avoid shouting or screaming, which is aggressive and makes you appear to have lost control.

Sometimes it may be more appropriate to lower your tone so as not to intimidate, but avoid sounding too submissive. Keep saying what you want or need to happen in a good-natured and fairly relaxed tone, until you get a response you are happy with. We feel confident, mentally alert and in control if we are physically stable and have plenty of oxygen in our lungs. Adopt an upright posture, with both feet firmly on the ground and breathe deeply. Mentally rehearse being assertive. Pick a specific situation, visualize it and run through it in your mind, rehearsing each part of what you want to say.

Remember you have options: you can choose to be assertive, submissive or aggressive, they are all part of you. It is very tiring to be assertive all the time, and you have the right to take a rest from it.

# RECOVERY FOLLOWING CONFLICT

After there has been some recognizable resolution to the conflict, it is important to consider recovery. This is more obvious when the conflict has spiralled into anger or violence, but it is essential for children who experience any feeling of abandonment as a revisiting of their primary abandonment and loss, and should not be ignored in other cases.

Relationship repair is moving on from damaging interactions, without pretending that they have not occurred. The child will need you to help repair the relationship and overcome the feelings of guilt, shame and failure that may follow conflict. Recognize and encourage their efforts to repair the relationship.

## Summative reflection

Summative reflection collects the child's main points (not yours) and key elements of the situation. This is the opportunity to address any outstanding issues that may be behind the conflict. It helps the child gain an integrated sense of what has happened, but is only helpful once calm.

# PROBLEM-SOLVING

Problem-solving is an important skill to acquire and to teach to young people. Life is inevitably full of problems and although it is irrational to assume that every problem can be solved, solutions or compromises can be found for most problems if time is taken to examine the deeper issues logically, creatively and thoroughly. It is important to take time to explore all the options.

Problem-solving can be seen as answering a series of questions. It is a cyclical process, as problem-solving steps may lead to beginning the process again. It is usually best to write the response to these questions. Writing helps to clarify thoughts and provides a record of ideas and solutions to which you can return from time to time for reassurance and clarification.

## Steps in problem-solving

In using a cyclical series of questions, some people find it helpful to write down the answers at each stage. The important thing is to be creative and imaginative in the early stages. Even 'daft' answers can lead to promising solutions.

1. What is the problem to be solved? Sometimes, identifying the problem is the key to the solution.

2. What is the ideal solution? Try to define what you would consider to be the ideal solution. Alternative solutions may emerge in the process of defining the ideal solution, and it is helpful to have as many alternatives as possible. Think as wildly as you like; it stimulates imagination.

3. What are the options? Think of possible ways of implementing the solutions identified in the previous step. Be as specific as you can about what you would do. You will drop some ideas as unrealistic, but some can be achieved.

4. What might happen if these options are put into practice? Make realistic assessments of the consequences of each option. Be realistic about painful or unwanted answers. Write down the consequences and face them no matter how difficult that might be in the first instance. It is possible to make considerable progress once reality is confronted. Mentally rehearse strategies and behaviours.

5. Make a decision. This is sometimes the most difficult step. You may want to draw on advice from trusted others. Having considered all the alternatives, make a decision. Don't procrastinate; you have enough information in the previous steps to decide. This will only aggravate the problem rather than solve it.

6. Act. Try out feasible solutions. If they don't work you've probably generated alternatives in earlier steps.

7. Evaluate. Has this worked? Failures or disappointments are necessary feedback in order to begin the problem-solving process again.

## Chapter Six

# Working with Anger

'Anyone can become angry, that is easy. But to be angry with the right person, to the right degree, at the right time, for the right purpose, and in the right way, this is not easy.' (Aristotle, *The Nicomachean Ethics*)

## LEARNING OUTCOMES FOR THIS CHAPTER

Once you have studied this chapter you should be able to:

- explain what anger is
- have insight into your own anger style
- understand the link between anger and unresolved separation
- promote change in anger styles
- understand triggers to anger
- maintain a low-stress environment
- demonstrate intervention skills appropriate to stages of the anger cycle
- intervene with an angry child in an understanding, effective, therapeutic and safe way
- ensure relationship repair after an anger outburst
- talk a child through an effective relaxation technique.

## HUMAN BEHAVIOUR

In order to explore and understand anger, it is useful to agree on some fundamental ideas:

- All people (including children) think, feel and behave.

- Behaviour, except when influenced in extreme ways by mental ill-health or drug use, means something, has a purpose and serves a need.

- We do not have conscious control or choice over all our behaviour.

- We respond to stimuli in ways that are either innate (instinctive) or learnt.

- Many of our learnt responses are so embedded in our behaviour that they are uncontrollable.

- Although children have different temperaments, and are born with emotional equipment to feel angry, they are not born with unhealthy ways of managing anger; they learn this from adults, or from children who have learnt from adults.

- All relationships go up and down and, for healthy development, children need to experience this safely.

Anger can be a response to frustration (an unmet need), but it can also be a release of pent-up emotion. Anger always has a trigger. The brain reacts and a combination of thoughts, memories and feelings of fear and threat is encoded and interpreted and response is looked for. The selection of a response is driven by the powerful experience of chemical changes in the body. What follows is an explosion of innate inner drives, physiological changes, and learnt patterns of behaviour.

## ANGER IN THE BRAIN

Anger is normal, natural and healthy. It is always a reaction to something and is part of the fight response to a perceived threat. When we perceive a threat we are biologically programmed towards fight, flight or freeze. The brain is flooded with hormones. It is part of our evolutionary development to produce these chemicals to enable us to act automatically in a way that preserves us from danger.

The human threat system can be seen as consisting of two parts, the amygdala system, that deals with the implicit emotional memory triggered by an emotional stimulus, and the hippocampal system that connects with explicit emotional memories about the emotional information. Threat is assessed when these two streams of emotional information are processed together in the frontal cortex.

Danger signals are received in an area of the brain known as the amygdala, which operates like the brain's alarm system, and generates states of mind that aid survival. Chemicals are released into the bloodstream that prepare the body for running and/or fighting, and flood the cortex so that we are thinking more instinctively (and more quickly) in ways that will promote survival in the face of the perceived threat.

In this state we are not thinking rationally. These chemicals cause the body to undergo dramatic changes: our pupils dilate, and awareness intensifies. Sight sharpens, impulses quicken, and our perception of pain diminishes. We are physically and psychologically prepared for fight, flight, or freeze, and are scanning and searching the environment for the enemy.

At the same time as tripping the chemical fight/flight/freeze response, the amygdala sends information to the pre-frontal cortex, the area of the brain associated with impulse control. Our conscious mind assesses the threat and if it downgrades it, it can control the impulse to take flight or to fight. However, this process requires a developed pre-frontal cortex. The pre-frontal cortex develops into adulthood, so children have less impulse control than adults, and during adolescence it is less effective at controlling impulses due to additional hormones present: adolescents have less impulse control than pre-adolescents. As insecure attachment is associated with poor frontal lobe development, anxiously attached children often lack impulse control. Experience hard-wires repeated patterns of behaviour into our brain: neurons that fire together, wire together, and so impulsive acts can become habitual.

## ANGER STYLES

Sometimes anger is a way of getting what we want (instrumental anger). For some hyper-aroused children, it can be a way of reproducing the high-octane environment that they have survived in until now. Anger can be very familiar, and even destructive anger can feel safe because it is familiar; it has become a habit. Individuals deal with anger in a number of ways, although one anger style may be dominant. Although our body releases certain chemicals that the mind detects and attributes to an emotional state when we are angry, the attribution we make depends on context. How we respond to highly aroused states is therefore governed by the situation we are immersed in. That is, how we react is context specific and influenced by circumstances. For example, you may be more ready to get angry with a close friend than with a physically powerful stranger. We are also more likely to express our anger badly if we are tired or stressed.

How we behave when we are angry depends on what we have learnt from others (perhaps unconsciously) as a way of expressing our biological response to a threat. It also depends on our beliefs about how we should or shouldn't behave, unconscious motivators, and individual difference in our temperament, personality and character. Some people shout loudly, cry, completely lose control, use verbal abuse, become physically aggressive, and damage property. Such anger responses may be ineffective as they lack control. Others have a strong tendency to avoid angry feelings, and become cold and overtly controlled, or they hope it will all go away, or perhaps they ignore it, but find themselves angry about something 'safe'. Their responses do not lack control, but may lead to 'leaked feelings' and it unlikely that their needs are being met. We can list five ways of dealing with anger:

- displacement (getting angry with something else)
- repression (unconscious anger)
- ineffective expression (problem anger)
- suppression (conscious choice)
- effective expression (healthy anger).

Displacement, repression and ineffective expression of anger can be seen as problematic, with damaging effects on our families, our friends, our communities, our society and ourselves. Displacement implies getting angry with a weaker or safer person, repression implies burying angry feelings that are too difficult to face. Problem anger is aggressive and destructive, turned outside on others or inside on the self. Children with poor self–other concepts are particularly prone to this. Suppression is a conscious choice to not be angry now. This is usually based on a sense of risk, and is an important social skill. It requires that we have inhibitors that we can call on in order to suppress the behaviour, and can control our impulse to act. However, we should be careful not to suppress anger to such an extent that it leaks out somewhere else.

We should also be good at expressing anger, able to be angry without feeling angry. It requires waiting until we are calm, valuing the other person's point of view, expressing our own feelings clearly and avoiding generalized comments and sweeping statements ('you always/never…'). It also requires that we offer solutions, reflect on our part and attitude, and avoid blame and exaggeration. In order to express anger effectively, it is helpful to distinguish between:

- what the other person did and the effects of their actions
- what I did and the effects of my actions
- how I felt
- what solution/change I would like.

## ANGER: A RESPONSE TO SEPARATION

Anger is a semi-automatic, psychological and biological response to the threat of separation. Commonly observed behaviour, like the parent who angrily scolds a toddler who runs into the road, shows us how angry, cohesive behaviour in the service of an affectional bond is both common and functional. This is the anger of hope. Anger shows the missing person that they were not there when they were needed, and makes separation less likely in future similar circumstances by discouraging the loved one from going away and by helping to overcome any obstacles to a reunion.

However, repeated, prolonged or permanent separations can produce anger of despair. Anger becomes dysfunctional when angry aggression crosses the narrow boundary between deterring separation and revenge; a strongly rooted affection laced with occasional anger is replaced by a deep-seated resentment, held in check by anxious uncertain affection. The most volatile anger of all is found in adolescents who not only experience repeated separations but also are constantly subjected to the threat of being abandoned. A painful internal conflict arises as the attachment figure arouses love, anger, anxiety and even hatred. The child becomes caught in a vicious circle as separation arouses hostility in the child, and hostility makes separation, rejection and abandonment more likely.

Disorganized attachment leaves the child without a coherent behavioural strategy for dealing with problematic intimacy. With no internal caregiving presence (the attachment figure held in mind) to soothe, their rage becomes directed towards their carers, both as a displacement activity and an attempt to be reassured that however extreme the behaviour, they will not be abandoned.

## CHANGE

Children with highly anxious and disorganized patterns of attachment cope with the hyper-arousal (unregulated emotions) that results from constantly feeling unsafe either through dissociation (shutting down the connections between thoughts, memories, feelings, actions and identity) or by being hyper-vigilant (constantly scanning for threats). They often show poor impulse control. Their 'catastrophizing self' predicts that all conflict ends in catastrophe, and leaves them in a state of hostile dependency. They are subject to an array of problems to which they can see no solutions. Memories, social cues and events are encoded in a distorted way, influenced by the IWM that predicts hostility and danger. Further, repeated experiences of the power of angry outburst can leave them addicted to anger. The low conflict environment provided by a therapeutic approach may be boring. It will take time and patience for them to learn to appreciate harmony and to establish self-regulation. All relationships go up and down, and these children need to experience this safely within therapeutic and supportive relationships. We should not be surprised by their anger, but we do need to survive it.

Is it reasonable to expect the child to lead the change? Their anger has probably protected them, empowered them, and made them feel better about their lives. They have modelled their anger behaviours on adults they have known. Change must come from us; we are their models now. We therefore need to consider how we deal with our own anger.

## SAEf CHARTS

An SAEf chart (Figure 6.1) is a direct observation tool that can be used to collect information about the setting conditions, triggers, events and reactions within a child's environment. They can be used for caregivers to think together about the child's triggers and responses, and help the child and caregivers make sense of the child's behaviour by unpacking the function that the behaviour serves for the child. The SAEf chart was inspired by the ABC chart, an idea developed by Felce and McBrien (1991), but takes a more functional perspective. That is, the analysis is intended to reveal what function the behaviour is serving for a child, what unmet need is being addressed, so that caregivers can focus on the unmet need rather than an unwanted behaviour. 'S' refers to the setting conditions: what was going on immediately before the behaviour: who was there, who was doing what, environmental factors (hot, cold, noisy, quiet, etc.), and internal factors (hunger, low mood, etc.)? 'A' refers to observed behaviour. This should be carefully described in terms of what the child did, so avoid general statements like 'He was violent' or 'He self-harmed'. Be specific: 'He kicked me in the shin' or 'He cut his left arm with the broken cup'. 'E' refers to the effects of these behaviours and events that immediately followed.

The 'SAE' is a process of factual recording. Once this has been done (one occasion may be sufficient, but you may need more) the caregiving group can meet to think together about the child and try to pick apart the incident. Whilst it may help to identify triggers, and allow plans to be adjusted to provide support to account for this, recognizing the function 'f' the behaviour is serving for the child (perhaps a temper outburst is helping avoid some unwanted task) is more likely to promote a therapeutic response. The same chart can be used to identify the drama triangle roles (see Chapter 3) that individuals may adopt, developing reflection and strategies to avoid becoming entangled in the child's relational history.

| Who was there? What were they doing? What was going on? | What did the person observed **DO?** | What happened as a result of these actions? | Discuss the purpose the behaviour may have served | What role was each person playing, if any? (victim, persecutor, rescuer) |
|---|---|---|---|---|
| **Setting conditions** | **Actions** | **Effect** | **Possible function** | **Person/role** |
| | | | | |

Figure 6.1: SAEf chart

# ANGER MANAGEMENT TRAINING

Many children display problem anger in social settings where mainstream social norms find such displays unacceptable, although in other cultural contexts, their display would be seen as normal. Contrast what is acceptable for a 15-year-old in school and what is acceptable for the same young person on an inner city estate. Their cognitive map is organized differently from general expectations, and they can benefit from learning how to organize their thinking to match mainstream society's expectations, learning how to apply different behavioural norms to the same feelings. Anger management training can encourage them to make better use of self-controls that they have, and learn new ones. However, traumatized children may lack the internal controls that this training requires. They may act impulsively, without much thought or self-control. They are likely to be experiencing hyper-vigilance, hyper-arousal and a catastrophizing self, and therefore find it difficult to learn new controls. Programmes that emphasis this learning are unlikely to be successful. Instead, these children need consistent and predictable responses will help them feel safe and begin to trust. Over time they can learn better ways of venting their pent-up frustration and anger.

## TRIGGERS

Stress is cumulative. Poorly attached children are likely to experience hyper-vigilance (being unable to relax, constantly scanning for threats), hyper-arousal (persistent, deregulated stress) and have poor impulse control. When we see accumulating stressors, we can be proactive in avoiding anger outbursts, sometimes by talking to the child, identifying stressors and empathizing with their feelings, sometimes by removing stressors (does a case review have to happen in the same week as a dentist appointment?)

In order to identify triggers, it is useful to record and monitor antecedents to behaviours. Recognizing triggers can allow caregivers to provide a low-arousal environment, and reduce overwhelming stress to manageable levels. Knowing what is soothing can allow us to provide safe stimulation.

However, avoidance is a poor strategy for dealing with anger. Because the child's anger is not situational, but is linked to early unresolved fear and separation, other triggers may emerge if we focus on the child recognizing and avoiding existing ones. In order to progress, the child needs to learn to recognize their feelings being triggered, and to recognize the impulse to destroy before acting on it. They need to learn other ways of expressing anger. In this they will watch us and model how we behave when we are angry.

## LOW-STRESS ENVIRONMENT

The planned environment is a relatively low-stress, low-arousal environment. This includes having predictable routines and maintaining a calm atmosphere in the home. However, when a child is becoming more aroused and beginning to lose their temper, we can help reduce the pressure and the feeling by ensuring a low-stress environment. Think about noise (music on, TV blaring) and audience (whether you can remove the audience of other children, reduce the number of adults, etc.)

## THE ANGER CYCLE

Anger follows a predictable cycle because it is biologically driven by the primitive fight or flight mechanism. Anger begins with a trigger, which is followed by a period of escalation towards an angry outburst. Some of us are less able to calm down during this escalation and may escalate more quickly than others. Unless the angry person is able to calm down there will be a crisis in which their pent-up emotion is released. Most of the damage done in an anger outburst is done during this crisis, and much of the work of managing anger is about surviving this storm of emotions without the relationship being damaged. Once the chemical energy of the flight/fight mechanism is dissipated, the angry person begins to calm down. At first they may not be truly calm, they may be on a kind of plateau of raised emotions where small triggers will set them off again. However, eventually they will calm down and usually enter a kind of post-crisis depression, in which their mood may be lower than usual. They are vulnerable at this point to feelings of self-loathing, and may defend against these feelings by further angry outbursts.

Understanding the cyclical nature of anger is a useful tool in managing anger. The skill in this situation is to apply the right techniques at the right time. The ability to assess where in this cycle the angry person is equips us to do just that. Some of the skills that are addressed below are specific to the parts of the cycle. To be good at managing anger is to be good at doing the right thing at the right time.

## PERVASIVE SHAME

The anger cycle always concludes with a period of post-crisis depression. The angry person's arousal level will always eventually drop below their general level. It has to, as the arousal is fuelled by fight/flight hormones, and an energy deficit is being created by the immense energy expenditure of the anger storm. The body needs up to 90 minutes to rest and recover before the ability to think clearly has returned. However, during this time the fuse can easily be re-lit. Two angry people will often reignite each other's fuses.

The insecurely attached and traumatized child is particularly vulnerable at this time. Lacking primary experiences of reintegrative shame, the child falls easily into a black hole of pervasive shame, with no hope of relationship repair or reattunement. This leaves the child with a stark choice. The anxious-avoidant child is vulnerable to despair, self-loathing and self-blame (leading to deliberate self-harm), whereas the anxious-ambivalent child, with nothing left to lose, is vulnerable to escaping this black hole by further acts of anger and violence.

Without sufficient experience of reintegrative shame, many children will escalate their anger cycle as a defence against the overwhelming feeling of shame; each shame-inducing outburst is defended against by another, more intense outburst, so that the child's threshold of anger-violence increases over time. The root of this, their poor primary experiences, is easily lost sight of, and the child is seen as angry, destructive and violent. The cure, adult punishment and coercion, is not seen as adding to the shame-based identity that is at the heart of the problem.

## EMOTIONAL FUNCTIONING UNDER STRESS

A child's ability to function well emotionally is related to their self-worth and security. Under emotional pressure, the child's emotional functioning may be significantly reduced. They may be prone to temper outbursts more commonly seen in very young children. It is not effective to reason with the child. A calm, empathic response is required. Avoid remarking to the child on their display of emotional immaturity, this may well feel like humiliation, but try to respond by comforting them as you would a much younger child. Emphasize messages of safety and belonging.

## MANAGING THE SITUATION

It is usually possible to predict to some degree how, why and to what extent a child will become angry. We can limit a child's ability to hurt us, and others, emotionally and physically. It also helps to be clear about what others expect us to do in response to the child's anger, and for the child to know these expectations. We should always try to communicate with the child, and in any group (including families) we need to be good at working together (watching out for each other's feelings). We can manage the situation by providing:

- consistency through rules, rewards, and sanctions that are relevant, reasonable and implemented by everyone using agreed criteria

- high expectations placed on behaviour and matched by rewards

- cohesion and promotion of a pro-social atmosphere through adults being fair, and holding to agreed values that are made explicit to the child

- constancy and a predictable environment, where changes are made gradually and in an evolutionary way, and adult attitudes to anger are also predictable

- satisfaction which is found in achievements, warmth and intimacy.

## WHOSE ANGER?

When faced with an angry person we can become angry ourselves. We may feel perfectly justified; after all, they are angry with us, they started being angry, we're just responding. Emotions are very powerful. The angry person's 'emotional brain' speaks directly to ours.

The problem is that this is not an effective way of dealing with anger. We started off with one angry person, and now we have two. We may not even be angry, but are perhaps experiencing the angry person's anger as our own, through a process called projective identification. Projective identification is a pre-verbal mode of communicating and relating. An infant cannot say how they feel, so instead makes the caregiver experience the same feeling. Later, the angry child projects a denied part of themself into the other person and ends up by powerfully controlling the receiver from within like a glove puppet.

Dealing effectively with anger requires us to first manage our own anger. Recognizing that we have absorbed the other's anger in this way helps us do this. There may be things that the other person is doing that it is perfectly justified to feel angry about. Now is not the time to deal with them. Effective expression of anger sometimes requires picking the time and place. Suppression is a conscious choice not to be angry now.

We ask our children to learn how to control their anger, but how well do we do?

## TRUST PROTECTION

Problem anger damages relationships and trust. It takes time to build both, and insecure attachment makes it hard to trust. When managing anger, the most important thing to achieve is to protect trust. The middle of an outburst of anger is not the time to deal with other issues; they may be important, but they can be dealt with when everyone has calmed down. Keep this in mind: I want to preserve trust; other goals can wait.

- Be assertive, but don't retaliate.
- Be careful what you say during the anger storm.
- Don't say anything you can't or won't fulfil.
- Listen with empathy.
- Keep responses child centred.

By protecting trust we protect the spirit of collaboration and co-operation that is essential in secure base experiences. The angry child gets locked into a familiar and repeating cycle. It is our role to get them out of it, not to be part of the problem. It is not the child's role to get the adult out of any familiar and repeating cycle that they have got caught up in. Adults should avoid escalating the situation by their response to the stimulus of the child's anger. They should also avoid backing the child into a corner, trying to win, and losing. Let the child know what you are doing, and why, emphasizing the benefits for them.

To enable the child to identify their own inner experience and to learn to communicate their feelings and needs, and recognize that others also have feelings and needs, we can communicate how the child's actions are making us feel. We need to be real about our feelings, and should not be frightened of expressing them to the child. However, the feeling tone should not enter our expression; we should express these feelings in a matter-of-fact tone of voice, that way the child learns that powerful feelings can be contained and can be safely talked about. We can use an assertive form of speech, such as 'When you...(*non-critical description of the child's acts*) I feel...(*accurate description of our real feeling*) because... (*honest appraisal of the reason, although this part can be omitted*)'.

- 'When you shout at me like this, I feel upset, because I always try to listen to you.'
- 'When you spit at me, I feel angry.'
- 'When you kick me, I feel hurt, because I am only trying to keep you safe.'

## ASSERTIVENESS AND THE ANGRY CHILD

Assertiveness does not back the other person into a corner, and allows them to preserve their dignity. It also allows us to preserve our dignity. As well as being assertive yourself, you need to encourage assertiveness in your child. Scary! Assertiveness is win-win. If the child can learn to be assertive, they are helping us win too. If they can deal with frustration, pent-up emotion and getting what they want assertively, they have less need and opportunity to get angry.

## ASSERTIVE COMMUNICATION

It is not just the content of what we say that counts; it is the way we put it across. It helps to:

- be honest with ourselves about our feelings
- keep calm and stick to the point
- be clear, specific and direct
- repeat our message whilst also listening to the child's point of view
- offer alternative solutions if there are any
- ask, when we are unsure about something
- if the other person tries to create a diversion, point this out calmly and repeat our message
- use appropriate body language
- always respect the rights and point of view of the other person.

### 'I' messages

When we are using assertive communication it is important that we speak for ourselves and avoid blaming other people. We speak for ourselves when we use 'I' messages, but when we use a 'You' message we can sound unempathic and blaming ('You never put you toys away. You leave your room in a mess for me to tidy up and you still want your pocket money'). However, we can re-phrase this as an 'I' message, clearly expressing how our feelings are affected by the other person's actions. We sound empathic and assertive ('When you don't put your toys away I feel angry and frustrated. Can we discuss what we are going to do about this before we talk about pocket money?').

## EARLY WARNING SIGNS

Although they are individual for each child, you may see some of these signs:

- physical agitation
- pacing
- fiddling
- changes in facial expression, eye contact, facial colouring and tone of voice
- verbal challengers
- rapid mood change
- over-sensitivity to suggestions or criticism.

## DE-ESCALATION

Once the child's anger has been triggered, the fight or flight system is triggered by a perceived threat and the child will escalate towards the anger storm. Early intervention can be effective because they are not yet fully aroused. However, the higher the arousal level, the less rational the person. It is important to avoid power/dominance body language. A calming hand gesture can be very effective. With an open palm at about chest height, make slow motions downwards with your hand as if patting the air, slowing each time. Avoid devaluing the other person by saying such things as, 'Pull yourself together', 'Don't be silly', 'Now don't start that', 'I thought you were more grown up than that'.

Faced with an angry child, we may well feel attacked, but our task is to open communication. This is best done by listening carefully. Hearing and valuing the child's opinions encourages their sense of being in control. Paraphrase what they have said, listening out for feeling words so that you can reflect feelings back to the child.

### De-escalation: listening skills

There are some basic things we can do to listen well:

- Be aware of personal space and body language. Don't appear threatening. Use body language that says you're involved and shows you're genuinely interested and listening.

- Try to stand in the child's shoes and try to view the things they are talking about from their point of view.

- Avoid saying 'I know how you feel'; you don't, you can't, and the child knows this.

- Encourage the child to talk by using simple, non-judgemental statements ('You seem quite upset').

- Reflect thoughts and feelings back to the child. Listen for feeling words and try to connect them to thoughts expressed by the child. ('You're telling me that you feel like **** because you think your mum hates you').

- Be aware of how you sound. Control the tone, pace and volume of your voice to show that you are remaining calm and in control.

- Ask a very few open questions: 'When?' 'What?' 'Who?' 'How?' 'Where?' 'Tell me...'. But avoid asking 'Why?' To answer requires giving reasons that the child does not have available at this time.

- Use attentive silence. It's OK not to speak. Wait calmly and let the other person say something more. It is important not to be uncomfortable whilst waiting. It can really help to say a simple phrase to yourself, so that the moment of silence passes more quickly for you (for example, silently saying, 'The healing power of silence').

- Be prepared with simple statements that demonstrate concern and offer choice: 'I'd like to help' or 'This has really upset you'. Follow with silence.

- Avoid telling the child to make choices. Commands are stressful and feel like threats.

- Listen carefully to the child's words so that you can give feedback that you recognize how angry the child is; be tentative: 'I can see you're really angry and upset, I think it's because...'

## Focused listening

Who is the focus of your listening? We can identify three ways we focus when we listen: 'me', 'we' and 'you'. Good listening has many benefits. As a listener, you feel you understand more of what is going on for the other person. They feel better for being listened to, and will probably not feel so alone. Good listening can help the other person clarify their thoughts and feelings, and it is a vital tool in the process of reconciliation. For most of us, 'me' and 'we' focused listening comes naturally. We move between the two levels as our attention or preoccupation changes. However, focusing our listening away from ourselves and very specifically onto another person is harder. 'You' focused listening requires practice.

### 'Me' focused listening

With 'me' focus, although I am listening to someone else, my main focus is on myself. The other person's words echo with my own preoccupations and I am relating everything to my experience. I am listening to get information for myself. This is not necessarily a bad thing, but it is important to recognize that 'me' focused listening is one-sided.

### 'We' focused listening

This is the everyday listening of good social interchange and everyday conversations, where we exchange facts and information. The focus is not just on me, but is on both of us.

### 'You' focused listening

The focus is no longer on me, or on both of us, but is purely on the other person. I am listening completely to you, and am not distracted by my own thoughts, which I need to put to one side.

## Showing acceptance

Acceptance is essential in secure base experiences. To demonstrate acceptance at times of anger, conflict and challenge is a powerful expression of unconditionality. Think of a time when someone was listening to you; how could you tell they were listening?

- They gave me focused attention.
- They showed they were interested in me.
- They gave good eye contact, which showed they were with me.
- They allowed me to have pauses when I was talking and did not interrupt.
- They showed that they cared about me through the expressions on their face and through their body language.
- They didn't rush off once I had started talking.

- They showed acceptance, and didn't judge me.

## De-escalation: talking skills

Important though it is to develop listening skills, we also need to consider how we talk to an angry person. Here are a few simple guidelines for talking effectively:

- Adopt non-threatening body language. Try not to assume a dominant position. Perhaps you can sit down (but keep yourself safe, angry people are unpredictable).

- Keep your voice calmer than theirs; speak slowly, do not shout. If they raise their voice, try lowering the volume of your voice, but don't mumble. Try lowering the register of your voice. Deeper voices may be heard more easily by a highly aroused child than a higher pitch.

- If you are trying to communicate instructions or choices, be sure that you use very simple language forms. It is easy for an angry person to misinterpret or mishear. Single words may be effective, for example calmly saying 'Language' may work better than 'Don't swear'.

- Try to concentrate on what they can do, avoiding telling them not to do things. Make commands instructions to do things, rather than not to. 'Sit here' is better than 'Don't go outside'.

## De-escalation: other strategies

Distraction or diversion is effective for younger children. It can help to relocate to a less stressful environment. Keep physical proximity, this maintains a sense of safety, but do not crowd the child or get close enough to present a threat. Try to find a way out for the child, perhaps by offering an alternative activity. Humour can help to de-escalate, but is a high-risk strategy. Humour is physiologically the opposite of anger and can be effective, but may be seen as belittling the angry person's concerns.

Don't escalate by getting angry as well. If we feel threatened we're likely to enter the anger cycle too, and may begin to feel punitive, or get involved in a power struggle. It is helpful to depersonalize the incident, after all it is probably not personal, although it may feel like it is.

## DURING THE ANGER STORM

If de-escalation does not work the child will eventually reach a crisis, and explode with anger. This is when the person has really lost their temper. Now we need to stick with them until they find it! If we abandon them, the insecurely attached child will re-experience previous feelings of abandonment, and they are likely to defend against these powerful feelings by becoming more hostile. During the anger storm, our task is to survive with trust in tact. In order to survive, we need to keep constantly in mind how the child is feeling.

Anger damages the physical and mental health of the angry person, their family life, friends and all those on the receiving end, the quality of relationships, property, and trust. It is the explosion of the anger storm that does most of this damage, and it is frightening and upsetting for all involved. However, the point at this time is not what the child may or may not be learning; it is to survive the damaging effects of anger with as little damage as possible.

During the anger storm avoid giving commands (they feel like threats, and therefore are likely to further escalate the situation). Don't try to distract or divert; for the child this feels as if their distressed state is not being taken seriously. Do not problem-solve, discuss or negotiate. These are complicated cognitive skills. In an aroused state such cognitive skills produce more challenge, further increasing the child's arousal and perception of threat. Don't use humour; it can feel like humiliation, and the child is likely to assume you are not taking their distress seriously.

In order to help the child, we need to first ensure that we manage our own feelings. Use empathic communication, and show the child that we will stick with them through this difficult time. Even if you move away, do so in a way that does not abandon them, as feelings of being left alone will become confused with other feelings of loss and abandonment, and further arouse the child's rage and sense of worthlessness. Show unconditional positive regard: the child is still valued and cared about and their feelings are recognized and validated.

The angry person cannot calm down. They are locked in a stimulus-response cycle and have probably learnt that things can only get worse. Angry, violent or unempathetic adults may have taught them unhelpful coping mechanisms or unacceptable behaviours. We can effect change through steam-valving.

## Steam-valving

Steam-valving is a powerful and simple technique that allows you to help the child release the exploding pressure of the anger storm in small, containable blasts. If the pressure of the child's anger is not released in a controlled way, it is likely to explode and damage relationships, people and property. Steam-valving allows you to not move with the force of the child's anger, although you may need to dance around a still point. Plan and practise empathetic statements that:

- allow the child to hear your empathy
- do not become a discussion
- avoid questions
- reflect truthfully how the child is feeling
- do not reflect side-taking or decision-making
- do not look like commands.

Don't move on from steam-valving until the person is calm (which may take longer than you think). The conversation might go like this. (Remember, all you are trying to do is not move from a still point in order that the pressure is released safely.)

> Child: 'It's not fair! Johnny hit me!'
>
> You: 'I can see you're angry and upset. I would be angry too, if somebody hit me.'
>
> Child: '***! You don't know how I feel!'
>
> You: 'I don't know how you feel, I can see you're angry and upset.'
>
> Child: '***! Aren't you going to do something about it?!'
>
> You: 'You seem angry and upset. We can talk about what to do later.'

Don't get drawn away from your 'still point' until the child has calmed down. They may continually try to draw you into negotiation, problem-solving, side-taking, controlling them, getting angry with them, and a whole host of other actions on your part that will damage the relationship whilst they are in this state. Steam-valving allows you to focus on their need to release the pressure. As they cannot be rational at this point nothing else is worth attempting. Because the crisis is biologically driven it will disappear if we don't feed it. As you feel the child pulling you away from this step, return to your original point as directly as you can without being threatening.

## When faced with violence

Anger easily turns to violence. If you keep a calm *persona* you stand a better chance. Use a non-threatening hand gesture: raise your open palm, fingers outstretched, but not tensed, to a little below shoulder height. Keep your elbow tucked in. Slowly lower you hand as if you are pushing air downwards. Exhale in order to free your body from fear paralysis, and say a simple command word such as, 'Wait' in a calm, but assertive manner. Bring the hand to about waist height, raising it just a little more quickly than you lowered it, and still slowly, to a point below where the gesture started, and repeat the movement three of or four times. You can also repeat the command word.

You have demonstrated that you are not a threat, but also that you are not a victim. This hand gesture can be used to back away from an assailant. Broadcast your actions, so that the other person knows you are not a threat, for example, if you want to get up and leave the room, 'I'm getting up now', 'I'm leaving now'. This can be combined with the hand gesture.

# PLATEAU

It takes time for the body to return to normal. During the plateau, it is easy to escalate the anger cycle by inappropriate intervention. The anger spikes may return for reasons inside the child (the original injustice, avoiding shame, a sense of power or powerlessness, etc.). The angry person feels vulnerable and confused. This is not a good time to get involved in anything other than lowering the level of arousal. Some tentative soothing nurture (perhaps a cold drink, a non-threatening enquiry into their welfare) and your safe proximity will help the transition to the next stage (recovery).

# RECOVERY

During the come-down of the recovery period, we can help the child recover from the effects of their temper outburst by lowering their arousal through soothing nurture; use warmth, reassurance and understanding.

## RELATIONSHIP REPAIR

Once the anger storm has passed, the trigger problem must be dealt with. We need to strike a balance between too much calming, seen as doing nothing, and being too quick to begin resolving issues, where we risk reigniting the fuse. Be aware of the risks present as the child enters the post-crisis depression. If the child has not had sufficient experience of reintegrative shame, they can feel abandoned and unable to re-establish attunement, falling into a black hole of pervasive shame.

It may take longer than you think before the child has calmed down. Once they are calm, again use listening skills. Acknowledge that the child is angry about something. Help the child solve the problem and deal with the perceived threat by getting a clear, factual account of what happened. Distinguish between behaviours that may be unacceptable and emotions, which are legitimate.

Once the anger storm has been weathered and everybody has survived, there may well be the issues that were there at the beginning and acted as triggers. The child may have a need to make amends for some of the unacceptable behaviour. Children need clarity. If you don't deal with the issues they may anxiously wait for them to resurface. Heightened anxiety can be a trigger. Don't blame, punish, criticise, or hold on to any resentment. Do problem-solve, give a sanction/ consequence for behaviours, not for feelings, if they are needed, but give them empathetically.

Role reversal work, where the child is encouraged to think about how the other person experienced their anger storm, can usefully be done at this time with some children. This requires a deal of skill and should be approached with caution. However, time spent unpacking some of the distorted thinking that fuels the child's sense of threat can be very productive.

### Reflective questioning

Reflective questioning is a powerful technique that can be useful during the relationship repair phase of the anger cycle. It makes an assumption that insight into and answers to the problem are within the child, and that they are most usefully drawn out not by supplying information, but through guided questions. We need to ask a series of open questions that prompt the child to the next insight. Avoid questions that begin with 'Why?' By gently asking questions and following replies with further questions we can allow the other person to open up to their own insights. It takes patience and practice; it also requires that we don't get dragged into giving answers. Whenever we begin to do so, we need to find another question. It can be slow. Just keep going, but push gently against the child's resistance. It's OK to stop if they become defended. You might even find yourself needing to steam-valve again, and the whole process starts again. But if you don't stop, eventually the child will join you. Be patient.

> 'That seemed pretty hard for us both. Do you know what made you feel so bad?'
>
> 'No.'
>
> 'Will you feel better if you don't talk about it?'
>
> 'Yeah.'
>
> 'How do you think I might feel if we do talk about it?'
>
> 'Angry.'
>
> 'Why do you think I'll be angry?'
>
> 'I might say things to piss you off.'
>
> 'What could you say that'd make me feel like that?'

## REAL ANGER MANAGEMENT: WHEN NOBODY IS ANGRY

Perhaps the most important work that is done in managing anger is the stuff we do when nobody is angry. That's partly in maintaining a total environment that has a clear purpose and understanding, and promotes trust in adult authority: adults are in charge and ensure safety. We should create an active community in which solutions can be negotiated, develop and maintain a culture of respect for children, adults, property, and difference, and ensure a calm, soothing, contained environment in which the adults set and maintain the emotional tone. As well as promoting a vision of the young people, staff and the agency as worth investing in and having valuable lives, we need to emphasize clear communication of feelings between adults and children to promote empathy, and acknowledge the child's perception of fairness and justice. Events need to be reframed in order to develop new, insightful narratives.

# RELAXATION

Children with anger problems or stress can benefit from learning how to relax. This is a very simple but powerful technique, which can be used by children as young as six but is probably more effective with older children. The idea is to tense each part of the body, note the feeling of tension/tightness and then relax/go floppy. This can be learned sitting in a chair, although some children may like to practise lying on beanbags. You need to adopt a soothing tone, speaking slowly and clearly. You can use your own words, but it goes something like this:

Sit comfortably, close your eyes, think of nothing.

Now make your hands into fists.

Really squeeze those fists.

Feel that tight feeling

Now relax.

Think of that lovely feeling of relaxation.

Make your hands into tight fists again and bring your hands up to touch your shoulders. Feel that tight feeling along your arms. Feel the tight feeling and relax, think of that lovely feeling of relaxation.

Now relax your arms, let them hang loosely by your side. Push your shoulders up and try and touch your ears. Go on, really push upwards. Feel that tight feeling in your shoulders. Feel the tight feeling and relax, think of that lovely feeling of relaxation.

This time scrunch up your face. Really scrunch up your face. Feel that tight feeling in you face and relax, think of that lovely feeling of relaxation.

Now make your tummy muscles tight. Really tighten those muscles. Feel that tight feeling. Feel the tight feeling and relax, think of that lovely feeling of relaxation.

Push your tummy forward this time, make your back arch, feel the tight feeling all along your back, feel that tight feeling, and relax, think of that wonderful feeling of relaxation.

Tighten the muscles in your legs, feel those muscles tightening, feel that tight feeling and relax. Feel that tight feeling along your arms. Feel the tight feeling and relax, think of that lovely feeling of relaxation.

Now make your toes into fists, really scrunch up those toes. Feel that tight feeling. Feel the tight feeling and relax. Think of that lovely feeling of relaxation.

Take a deep breath, hold that breath, feel that tight feeling in your lungs, feel the tight feeling. Let the breath out slowly and feel all the tightness go away. Think of that lovely feeling of relaxation.

Keep your eyes closed. We are going to check each part of your body to see if there is any tightness. Think of your hands and arms and if there is any tightness just let go of it. Now check your shoulders, neck and face. If you find any tightness just let go. Check your back and shoulders, your legs and feet. If you find any tension just let go.

You should now be feeling wonderful and relaxed. Just enjoy that wonderful feeling and when you feel ready open your eyes.

## An alternative method

Lie on your back on the floor, neck, back and legs in a straight line, arms by your side. Close your eyes and imagine that you have left a grey, overcast day behind, and are lying on a beach in the warm sun.

Breathe out, and watch your breath push the grey day out of your lungs, breathing in, and feel the warm yellow sunshine filling your lungs.

(*Repeat a few times.*)

Breathe out...and breathe in, feel the warm sun flowing down to your toes, warming them, making them go soft and floppy.

Breathe out...and breathe in, feel the warm sun flowing down to your lower legs, warming them, making them go soft and floppy.

Breathe out...and breathe in, feel the warm sun flowing down to your upper legs, warming them, making them go soft and floppy

Breathe out...and breathe in, feel the warm sun flowing down to your tummy, warming you, making you soft and floppy.

Breathe out...and breathe in, feel the warm sun flowing down to your hands, warming them, making them go soft and floppy.

(*Repeat for arms, chest, shoulder, neck, and face.*)

Just lie here in the sun, breathing in and breathing out. When you feel ready, slowly open your eyes. Don't move for a moment. Lie there for a moment, then slowly sit up and breathe out.

# EXERCISES

Below is a series of exercises to practise some of the key skills discussed above. Some can be done alone; for others you will need a trusted partner.

## Exercise: body language

With a partner try different types of posture and body language as you imagine being the aggressor, the victim and finally an assertive person. Your partner plays the opposite role of passive versus aggressive and so on. Finally, see what it feels like to change from being in a passive or aggressive stance to using assertive body language.

Just standing in a confident, calm way can feel empowering.

## Exercise: steam-valving

The child says, 'It's not fair! Johnny hit me!' I can say, 'I can see you're angry and upset. I would be angry too if somebody hit me'. Work out a step-by-step conversation where the adult follows the principles set out in the 'steam-valving' section above.

## Exercise: assertive communication

Even though you want to be empathetic there are two people in these difficult events. To be assertive you need to let the other person know how you feel. You must be genuine about your feelings. Using the examples below, try to find a response for the adult that takes the form, 'When you...I feel...because...'

- The child spills washing up liquid all over the floor.

- The child does all her homework.

- The child hits another child.

- The child runs out into the road.
- The child swears at you.

## ANGER MANAGEMENT WORKSHEETS

Figure 6.2 shows excerpts from a series of anger management worksheets.

- Level 1: Explain several scenarios and ask the child to colour or draw on a face that best expresses their feeling. Start with positive things; move on to more difficult ones. Go at the child's pace, balancing challenge and support. You might say, 'Draw how you feel when you get your pocket money. Now draw how you feel when I ask you to make your bed. Now draw how you feel when Rachel calls you a name'.

- Level 2: Start with something the child enjoys, a favourite activity or pastime. Develop towards actions that are associated with anger events. Although three steps are shown here, use what you need (but if you're going over seven steps, ask yourself who is being avoidant).

- Level 3: Now you are helping the child to reflect on how their feelings influence their behaviour. Again, start with something enjoyable, take as many steps as the child needs, but keep in mind the observation about avoidance.

- Level 4: Now you are helping the child link their feelings to their thoughts. Distorted thoughts can be challenged through reflective questions: see 'Unblocking techniques' section in Chapter 4.

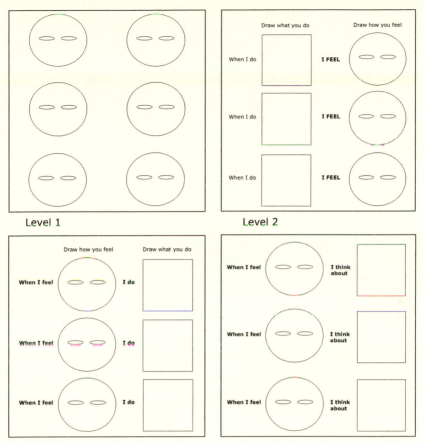

Figure 6.2: Anger worksheets

## Chapter Seven

# Managing Challenging Behaviour

Strategies can be successfully employed within a planned environment to work effectively and therapeutically with a range of challenging behaviours. These approaches help contain the outward manifestation of the poor primary experiences in an authoritative style, in a safe and positive way that preserves trust and works towards a positive outcome. The emphasis is understanding that behaviour is communicating something to us that needs to be understood, and on developing adult thinking that promotes understanding of the child's perspective to safely hold their uncontainable emotions, allowing a safe space for recovery.

## LEARNING OUTCOMES FOR THIS CHAPTER

Once you have studied this chapter you should be able to:

- place challenging behaviour in a wider social context
- use challenging behaviour as an opportunity to promote secure base experiences
- respond to attachment needs early and reduce the child's dependence on maladaptive coping
- contribute to preventing the cycle of coercion
- help a child understand what keeps a problem going
- look for the communication in the child's behaviour
- assess the effectiveness of intervention options
- respond effectively to affective and instrumental aggression
- respond effectively to the passive-aggressive child
- use effective verbal communication skills, including reflective and assertive approaches
- apply effective parenting skills to challenging behaviour.

# CHALLENGING BEHAVIOUR

The term 'challenging behaviour' refers to a range of behaviours that present a problem to others, not something intrinsic to the individual. Challenging behaviour usually refers to verbal and physical aggression, over-excited behaviours that are difficult to control, constant repetitive behaviours and self-harm. These behaviours need to be of a frequency, intensity and duration that threatens the physical safety of the person or others, or limits the person's access to ordinary community activities.

All forms of challenging behaviour are significant and need to be addressed, as they can and do affect the quality of the child's life, and the lives of the adults who care for them. Rather than seeing the child as a difficult person, the challenge is to understand that children with the most challenging behaviours are likely to have the greatest unmet needs. There is a cause for difficult behaviour, and that cause is rooted in the circumstances of the individual's life.

Behaviour usually has a reason; our challenge is to uncover what that reason is. Behaviours are strengthened when they are rewarded and/or are effective. However, the nature of reward is individual, and some of the things adults see as disincentives can be experienced as a reward by the child. Problem behaviour can also be due to a lack of inhibition and control. Children who have seen violence or been the victim of violence may resort to violence themselves. Children may also be behaving at their emotional or developmental age, which may be significantly lower than their chronological age. There may be transference of angry aggressive feelings as a result of an over-identification between two people; this can be happening, for example, when the anger a child feels towards their mother is transferred to a female worker.

Over-excited behaviours that are difficult to control, and repetitive behaviours, are effectively managed through a carefully planned environment and an authoritative approach to parenting. It may also be useful to use some traditional behaviour management techniques, and the way these can be applied to an attachment-focused model of care is discussed in Chapter 8.

Age-inappropriate sexualized behaviour, often seen as reactive to early sexual abuse, and self-harm present serious challenges to carers. However, detailed consideration of these is not possible within the available space of this book. However, the over-arching principles of the therapeutic approach and the planned environment laid out here are an effective starting point for helping young people who show these difficulties. It is important to recognize that self-harm should never be seen as attention seeking (which does not mean the child does not need attention) and that sexualized behaviour may indicate sexual abuse, but there are other explanations. Understanding the reasons why a child acts a certain way does not mean accepting unacceptable behaviour, unacceptable behaviour is just that, unacceptable, but understanding can help influence change.

None of us is the only one to face challenging behaviour. In the process of surviving the tragic circumstances of their lives, the children we work with have often learnt many things that are difficult for us to deal with. It is fair to say that they have learnt these things either from adults or from other children, who have learnt them from adults.

In order to recover from the damaging effects of their learnt behaviours, these children need adults who are good at managing their own feelings, and able to manage their responses to the child's behaviours. When coping ourselves with the difficulties these children bring with them it is worth reflecting on what they may be learning from us about how to cope with difficulty, and to keep a sense of perspective.

## CHALLENGE OR OPPORTUNITY?

When caring for a deeply troubled child the times when things are going well are precious, and over time may become more frequent, but it is the times when things are difficult and we face the challenge of the child's disturbing behaviour that provide rich opportunities for recovery. Some children display repetitive and persistent anti-social, aggressive or defiant behaviours, which may include violence to others, destruction of property, theft, deceitfulness, and serious refusal to follow rules.

Children learn. The natural, healthy course of a child's development takes the totally dependent infant to a fully interdependent adult. This developmental pathway is blocked by highly insecure or disorganized attachment and early trauma. Much difficult and challenging behaviour is attachment behaviour that is being expressed in a pathological way. Attachment behaviours are switched on by fear and danger and are switched off by safety. For hyper-vigilant and hyper-aroused children there is little experience of safety and they have developed behaviours that will bring adult proximity, even though the proximity may be resented (a kind of hostile dependency).

If adults can respond consistently and predictably over time, to the child's attachment needs for proximity, safety and sensitive caregiving before the child's behaviours switch on in such a way that adults are forced to meet the child's attachment needs on the child's terms, the child begins to experience needs being met as they arise, not because they are coercing adults to meet them. Over time, the child's dependence on maladaptive coping reduces, trust and security develop, and the child's pathological and coercive attempts to get their attachment needs met diminish. This is emotionally demanding work for caregivers and others, because it requires that we endlessly look to satisfy the child's needs before they are overtly expressed through disturbing behaviour, but it is not as wearing as the inability to survive the child's challenging behaviour. Over time, as trust and predictability develop, the need to be so pro-actively responsive diminishes.

Whilst clearly specific behaviours do need to be addressed, the underlying approach to addressing challenging behaviour that is taken here acknowledges that children learn though observing and modelling others, and encourages a psychosocial environment and interpersonal dynamic that builds and supports communication and the mutual understanding of emotions, whilst developing the skills needed to address the causes of problem behaviour.

The child's internal working model (IWM) predicts hostility or abandonment as a direct result of conflict. The IWM is what the individual knows. It is both comfortable and familiar, and although it causes pain and suffering, the child is drawn to events that trigger these thoughts and feelings by their familiarity.

We are presented with a dilemma, to focus on extinguishing (or reducing) unwanted behaviours, or to answer unmet primary needs, expressed as difficult behaviour, in order that the child no longer needs to behave in such a way in order to get their needs met. In order to work therapeutically with challenging behaviour, we need to do both, so that the child is provided with opportunities to grow towards being an autonomous, self-regulating individual. The child cannot simply remember some qualitatively different relationship from that embedded in their IWM, they can only experience it in their relationships in the here and now. If we can respond to their challenging behaviour in such a way that we meet their attachment needs, the experience challenges the construct of the IWM and promotes the cognitive restructuring essential for recovery.

The child's behaviour may get worse before it gets better. As the child begins to trust a relationship as a secure base, they will need to test this out, through their actions asking the caregiver, 'What do I need to do for you to reject me?' The task is to stick with the child, showing warmth, providing explanation and maintaining expectations, so that the security of the relationship is enhanced in these encounters, as the child realizes that relationships go up and down and the developing relational bond survives.

This is a difficult task and requires insight, reflection, self-control and sacrifice; in at least that we need to be able to give up our intuitive right for revenge and retaliation. Any individual who is attacked is likely to feel the need for some form of retribution, but we must also realize that it is not effective. The child expects nothing more; it is in our refusal to retaliate and our insistence that the child's attachment needs are met, that the gloomy prediction of the child's IWM that the other is hostile and the child is worthless is eroded, and gradually replaced with trust and a sense of worth.

Challenging behaviour requires us to respond in an authoritative way, which balances adequate care with appropriate control. We should be clear what our expectations are, and as far as possible these should be framed in what we'd expect the child to do:

- 'I expect you to be in at the proper time tonight' is better than 'Don't be late'.

- 'I know you can tell me the truth' is better than 'Don't tell lies'.

- Expectations are more powerful if accompanied by an explanation: 'I expect you to be in at the proper time tonight, you need to get up in time for school tomorrow'.

Expectations and explanations need to be accompanied by genuine warmth. A distinction can be made between child-centred and child-directive approaches. Although children are individuals and some children require a more directive approach than others, some directive approaches should clearly never be used. Even if we are being directive, we can still do so in a relatively child-centred way, for example, it is sometimes necessary to give commands, but we should still pay attention to the child, and praise them for complying. Teaching is directive, so we should also remember that children learn through participation, and that fun and playfulness are useful ways for children to learn. Child-centred approaches include praise, giving attention, giving warmth, showing interest, describing sights, events and memories, listening, joining in with the child's activities, playfulness and fun, doing with, rather than leading, and participatory learning. Child-directive approaches include giving commands and instructions, criticism, unclear messages, making threats, telling off, instructing, directing and teaching, using ridicule, being aloof, and telling rather than doing. This is not to say that it is never good practice to be directive. Children need directions, and adults also need to be skilled at being directive whilst remaining calm, encouraging collaboration and avoiding power struggles.

## COERCION CYCLE

We bring our relationship history with us. Over-controlling, punishing parenting does not encourage children to comply. Instead, the child feels angry and rebellious ('If I must, then I won't'). Powerless, inadequate and absent parenting leaves the child feeling out of control, terrified and abandoned.

Angry, rebellious children can make professionals feel powerless and inadequate, the result of which is that the child now feels out of control. The inability of professionals to exert appropriate control makes the child feel terrified at their own power and left alone to deal with its effects (abandoned). Often the intuitive response is to attempt to regain control through punishment. The child is caught in a cycle of coercion that cannot change the underlying problems, but instead reinforces the bleak inner world of worthlessness and hopelessness. The acting-out child is no longer just a lad but is seen as, and treated as, deeply bad.

The neglected child is also at risk from this cycle of coercion. The absent parent has left the child feeling out of control; as their behaviour escalates (often into harming themselves) concerned adults can become over-restrictive, and revert to strategies that feel to the child as if they are being punished. The child becomes less compliant, 'If I must, I won't', and professionals feel powerless in the face of the child's collapse.

This cycle of coercion is deeply worrying for carers, who can feel overwhelmed by the child's turmoil, and the difficulty in selecting effective interventions. The adult's alternative strategy is to be neither authoritarian in the face of the child's being out of control, nor absent in the face of their rebellion, but to provide authoritative parenting. This is not easy. The child's powerful feelings and behaviours exerts influence on their developmental niche, recreating their past experiences of relationships in the here and now of well-meaning care.

# WHAT KEEPS A PROBLEM GOING

The child's problem behaviour is sustained by five factors that are interconnected to, and reinforce, each other: thoughts, mood, behaviour, physiological changes and environment. The child's thoughts and metal images are linked to their internal working model and distorted schemas. Thoughts of worthlessness, lack of trust, lack of effectiveness etc. dominate and filter out experiences that may give rise to other thoughts than feelings of worthlessness, anger or despair. Influenced by trauma and poor primary experiences, the child has poor quality mood and unregulated feelings, which can give rise to further negative experiences, which the child thinks are a result of their bad feelings about themselves ('I feel bad, so bad things happen') and further sustain the problem.

Behaviours become entrenched and habitual, but they also shape relationships. Hostile aggressive behaviours, or withdrawal and avoidance, keep other people at arm's length, and confirm the distorted self-belief and negative feelings that underlie the problem behaviour. Biological changes that are experienced as part of the problem can also be reinforcing: angry, aggressive children experience an adrenaline rush that sustains the problem behaviour, the child feels a sense of release, and thinks they are bad and powerful, further sustaining the problem behaviour. The environment in which the child is living, and the wider systems in which they operate, entrenched family culture, poor professional practice, anti-therapeutic care, some peer groups, anti-social merging in the care system, all sustain problem behaviour. This network of self-sustaining elements also provides opportunities for recovery. By making improvements in one element, we influence the others. Change is promoted through understanding how these elements influence each other.

We have already examined the therapeutic changes that can be achieved in a planned environment. The child's biological state can be improved through good primary care, good diet, exercise and sufficient sleep. When we consider challenging behaviour, we are also concerned with the linkage between thoughts, feelings and behaviours. How we feel influences how we think (e.g. in a low mood, we are more likely to have negative thoughts), and how we think influences how we feel (e.g. if we think we are being threatened we feel afraid). Both thoughts and feelings influence how we behave (e.g. if we think we've been wronged and we feel angry, we may get revenge), and our behaviour directly influences our thoughts and feelings (e.g. if we stumble into someone and feel upset if we've hurt them).

# INNER WORLD OF THE CHILD

## The child's communication: emotions

Basic human emotions are universal and innate, selected in the course of evolution as useful signalling behaviours. Infant and adult emotional expressions correspond. The distinctive nature of various emotions means that they figure predominantly in a child's ability to communicate need, and to establish a bond with others. Adults are able to accurately read (and respond to) children's emotional states. Emotions are therefore an important part of the language of children. Talking about and discussing feelings with the child helps develops emotional literacy and empathy. It is essential to validate a child's emotions at the same time as being clear that unacceptable behaviour is unacceptable. (It is OK to be angry, but it is not OK to hurt someone/break things because we feel angry.) The child needs a clear and consistent message that, 'There is nothing so terrible it cannot be talked about'.

## The child's communication: behaviour

Behaviour can be functional, for example acting a certain way may get me out of a stressful situation, or it may be about a lack of control, just blowing a fuse because that's the point that I have reached. Behaving is also an important method of communicating. Think of the way a cat tells a human that it needs feeding, or a dog asks to go for a walk. Not all our behaviour is rational and intentional. The way someone behaves is tied up with their thinking and their feeling. Thinking and feeling are influenced by early experiences. There is no point in becoming angry when faced with disturbing or challenging behaviour; it is better to ask ourselves: 'What does this behaviour mean?'

Behaviour also causes communication. How we (and the other person) communicate by behaviours, significantly influences the messages we receive alongside the words. In trying to understand the communication implicit in behaviour, it is useful to consider whether we (or the other person) has difficulty in expressing thoughts. If it is difficult to express thoughts we are more likely to rely on our behaviour (for example, compare how we express our anger through our behaviour when it is easy to say something, and when it is not).

A human infant is biologically programmed with attachment behaviours that can bring about safety. When a child has not experienced satisfactory reunion following separation they experience a pervading sense of loss (of the attachment object). For Looked After children, this sense of loss is frequently compounded by separation from home, loss of place in the family, loss of siblings, peers and extended family.

The insecurely attached child will frequently display attachment behaviour, triggered by their inner insecurity, in situations in the socio-emotional environment that would not trigger attachment behaviour in a securely attached child; hyper-vigilance and hyper-arousal distort their perception of danger. If the child's attachment is disorganized, they will have no organized representation of significant adults, and their behavioural attempts to find safety will be either chaotic or controlling.

## INTERVENING

Removal of environmental stress and improving the quality of the child's and carers' interpersonal, day-to-day life is the best place to begin. However, the child should not be forced to be close to adults; closeness needs to be learned and the child needs the opportunity to develop trust.

### Assessing interventions

Interventions that might work can be chosen on the following basis and these factors need to be taken into account:

- What has worked before?
- What is likely to be at the root of the problem that requires intervention?
- What are the antecedents to the behaviour?
- Who is available?
- Someone else may offer a more effective response.
- Support may be required.
- If the child is relatively unknown there may be something from previous experience that gives a hint.
- Is it really necessary to intervene?
- Whose problem is it?

- What are the planned, agreed interventions?
- What level of intervention is appropriate?
- The safety of everybody affected needs to be considered.
- Is there a risk to self, others, or of serious damage to property?

Individuals will contribute to therapeutic programmes if there is a good degree of trust, they are motivated to change, and they are empowered to contribute by their views being sought at the beginning. Motivation is more likely if they have been involved in deciding what needs to change and how that change is brought about, and they are consistently given a voice and are listened to. This is demonstrated to them when their comments are actively sought and are obviously valued. It is helpful to establish a feedback process for them to give comments at the beginning.

## Managing challenging behaviour

When things are getting out of control, control the things that you can, and don't worry about the things that you can't. Remember, you may need to act to keep safe. We should endeavour to set the emotional tone, so that the child does not learn that their behaviour is powerful enough to manipulate adult emotions. The message to the child is that adults are in control and keep everyone safe.

- Keep ourselves calm, be predictable in our attitudes.
- Keep in mind how the child is feeling.
- Avoid sweeping generalizations.
- Work out consistent responses ahead of problems, avoiding becoming coercive.
- Don't enter into battles we can't win.
- Leave a way out, with dignity and choice.

# AGGRESSION

A definition of aggression that provides a working basis for further thinking can be usefully summarized in three points:

- Aggression is the delivery of harmful acts by one person on another.
- These harmful acts are intended to harm the victim.

- The aggressor expects that the harmful acts will have their intended effects.

Blurton Jones (1972) observed that adults were not always good at distinguishing acts of childhood aggression from rough and tumble play. As well as demonstrating that adults are often poor judges of children's aggression, from observations of groups of children in the playground he identified features of aggression that could be differentiated from 'rough and tumble' play. Aggression was seen as frown, fixate, hit, push and 'take-tug-grab'. In contrast, in rough and tumble play children showed a 'laugh-playface', and tended to run, jump, hit-at, and wrestle.

Writers on human aggression usually distinguish between the affective and the instrumental. Affective aggression is accompanied by strong negative emotional states. Anger usually instigates then guides affective aggression, the main aim of which is injury or harm to the provocateur. However, behaviour does not need a strong emotional basis to be aggressive. The primary aim of such aggression is not the injury of the victim; the aggression is simply the means to some other desired end. This is referred to as instrumental aggression. Although this distinction is not conceptually clean, it is useful in tracing the developmental course of aggression. And as these forms of aggressive acts represent different emotional states and different motivations, it can be very helpful to work out what form of aggression is being dealt with.

Insecurely attached children may have poor regulation of emotion. The long-term intervention for affective aggression with this group of children is to work on their impulse control, emotional regulation, internal working model, attachment patterns and empathy.

A child who uses instrumental aggression has learned that this behaviour is effective. Assertive conflict resolution, firm boundaries and clear consequences, so that the behaviour is not rewarded, together with learning other ways of having reasonable demands met, is effective in such cases. Many children will show both behaviours at different times. Unpicking this is difficult but necessary.

An individual's aggression is fairly stable over time, although there are some important developmental changes that take place during childhood, and in general a reduction in amount of aggression through the course of childhood. Although the amount of aggression displayed decreases over age, the reduction is almost entirely in instrumental aggression that has no aggressive motive. There is generally an increase in aggressive acts among boys from age nine to 14. Sex differences at this age may be linked to the way aggression is manifested. Boys of this age use confrontation, whereas girls use more subtle forms of aggression such as ostracism and alienation.

There is also a developmental change in the type of aggression used. Physical aggression reduces as age increases: two-year-olds hit, but ten-year-olds also use humiliation, sarcasm, teasing, etc. Situations in which a child reacts aggressively also change with age. In early childhood, aggression is nearly always with other children, mostly in disputes over possession of toys. However, aggressive acts increasingly involve parents and disputes over routines. In later childhood group membership begins to play a part. Although children also fight as part of a group, increasing cognitive development brings greater control. It also brings greater opportunity to plan aggressive actions and make them more effective.

Although individual differences in aggression are a fairly stable trait, this does not mean that it cannot be influenced by experience. To some degree, levels of aggression reflect acquired problem-solving strategies. Children who learn good pro-social problem-solving are unlikely to learn aggression.

Rather than the situation itself, an individual's action is determined by a series of interpretative and decision-making stages. Social cues, goals and memories are encoded and interpreted before a response is selected and acted upon. Individuals will perceive similar situations differently; aggressive children may overreact to ambiguous signals, and more readily select aggressive responses, receiving hostility or rejection in return. Aggression may result from quite different processes in individuals, for example, a deficit in social skills or an internal bias in attitudes to others, events or situations.

For children with poor attachment, the IWM predicts hostility and interference. This prediction inhibits the search of a response and influences the selection of a response. The consequences that arise from their choice of response adds to memories that inform the next cycle, and either confirm or challenge the IWM. Non-aggressive responses to the child's aggression promotes cognitive restructuring; aggressive responses fulfil the prophecy and reinforce the IWM.

## PASSIVE-AGGRESSIVE CHILDREN

Many highly insecurely attached children fear dependency and intimacy, and develop a powerful need to control others. Often out of touch with their feelings, with poor self-image and low self-esteem they may be guarded and mistrustful or fear competition due to feelings of inadequacy. They take on a victim role, and blame other people for their situation, feeling disempowered and unable to change things. This can result in a behavioural style usually described as passive-aggressive. Instead of being openly hostile, they are highly evasive and avoid addressing their problems, usually through sulking and unspoken threats of aggression. Passive-aggressive behaviour is associated with avoidant attachment (organized and disorganized). They are likely to show a consistent pattern of exerting no effort toward improving their relationships, and avoid discussing unpleasant topics, often denying problems exists when all the evidence points to the opposite.

The passive-aggressive child can make us feel very unsafe and their high avoidance backed up with unspoken threats of violence, can trigger avoidance in caregivers. However, it is the child's fear that triggers this. They need to feel safe, and to have their self-esteem nurtured. It is important that caregivers recognize that the child is afraid of conflict because they do not want to lose the relationship. Caregivers need to be assertive, open and honest, and able to admit their negative feelings and anger. It is important to be direct, but show them that you respect, value and trust them: 'I ain't going to lie to you, this is a problem when you bang doors like that'. Always leave the passive-aggressive child a way out (they may have to avoid any assertive response), but address issues when they arise. If they are left, the aggressive defence builds.

The child needs opportunities to express their feelings. Let them know that you really want to know how they think, and that you can empathize with their feelings. It will take time, but if you stick with the child they will begin to trust the relationship sufficiently to open up.

When avoidance or passive-aggression does not work the child falls of the edge into a dark abyss: no longer being able to cope with avoidance or control the other person through suggested threats. At this point the child may erupt into an uncontrollable rage, turned either inwards on themselves or outwards on other people or property. At this point the child needs us to be very calm, unmoved by the outbursts. It helps to remind ourselves that this is their problem, not ours, and our role is to help, not to become responsible for another person's behaviour. Calm, assertive messages, and the continued provision of emotional and physical safety are required.

## WORKING WITH VIOLENCE

Affective violence is often triggered by fear, which may be driven by false beliefs about others' intentions or motives, feelings of humiliation, which can include a lack of choice and loss of control for an individual over their own life, or frustration, which may be associated with a lack of skill to deal with the situation an individual finds themselves in.

We are the single most important factor in minimizing the escalation into violence, when we are faced with an angry or aggressive child. We therefore need to acquire good practice skills. We need to be self-aware, that is, able to acknowledge our own levels of stress and anxiety.

We need a choice of approaches to deal with violence. Giving personal space keeps us safe and prevents crowding the child, who may feel under threat. Keep at arm's length, and if the child intrudes into your space, back off. It can be helpful to be at the same level, which might mean sitting down to lower your height and reduce the perception of being a threat. Don't make sudden moves, ensure that gestures and movements are overt and not open to misinterpretation. Open gestures, hands within sight and palms open will demonstrate that you have nothing to hide. Personalizing yourself, and emphasizing co-operation, protects you from becoming a victim. Encouraging the child to see you as a person, not just part of the system, will encourage responsibility. By emphasizing your willingness to co-operate, you are demonstrating your willingness to work with the child to solve the problem. Talk clearly, and do not talk more loudly than the angry person. If you lower your voice, the child may not hear you, and misinterpret or become frustrated, but if you shout, you will appear aggressive. Tone of voice is also important. Don't argue, even if you're right; arguing only leads to raised voices on both sides, and is likely to increase anger, frustration and humiliation. Offer solutions, but do not make unrealistic promises. Just because the child's behaviour is unacceptable, this does not mean that they do not have a genuine concern. When the situation is resolved, there will be ample time to reflect with the child on how they dealt with their anger or frustration. It is also important to manage others. Having others around may raise levels of arousal. If possible, have them move away.

The ways in which we respond are shaped by our own past experiences, and beliefs we hold about ourselves. By recognizing and challenging our underlying assumptions, we can broaden our repertoire of approaches. Table 7.1 contrasts unhelpful assumptions that we can make when we feel threatened with more helpful alternatives.

**Table 7.1: Beliefs about ourselves**

| Unhelpful assumptions | More flexible alternatives |
|---|---|
| I should take control. | How do I enter into negotiations? |
| I must never run away. | I need to avoid a confrontation that would make the situation worse. |
| I must never show fear. | Fear is a normal response to these situations. It's not only me who feels afraid. |
| I shouldn't back down to threats. | This is not personal. How do I find out what the child's problem is? |
| They're stronger than me. | The use of personal power/strength can make things worse. It is the skills I can use that matter. |
| I should know best what to do. | It's OK not to know. |

# DECEITFULNESS

Children who steal, lie, or are highly dishonest present another challenge for caregivers. Stealing can be a response to peer group pressure, a way of getting things they want or feel they need (make-up, cigarettes, sweets, etc. are often stolen for this reason). Stealing may also be for excitement, revenge or spite. Some children steal to have a plentiful supply of items to buy friendship. Often these behaviours are rooted in the same developmental difficulties as other challenging behaviour: low self-worth, insecurity, a lack of feeling effective, not feeling valued, wanted or belonging anywhere. It is important not to over-react to these challenging behaviours, and to avoid negative criticism, labelling or a highly punitive approach. As with all challenging behaviour, the essential thing to get right is the authoritative approach (high explanation, expectation and warmth). If you wish to use consequences, they need to be proportionate, fairly immediate and over reasonably quickly. If the child is confronted and supported, through good explanations and genuine warmth, over time they begin to experience the emotional safety of being unconditionally regarded, boosting the child's sense of belonging and self-worth.

- Be clear about rules and expectations.

- Explain why they should not steal, lie, or be deceitful.

- Show genuine warmth and unconditional positive regard.

- Show the child that you trust them.

- Set a good example: don't lie or be deceitful yourself.

These behaviours can also be habitual, and we need to acknowledge that a single event is more easily responded to than deeply entrenched behaviour. Intervention is most likely to be effective if we understand the triggers, any naturally occurring consequences (popularity, smoking, money) and the function the behaviour serves for the child. Our response can be helped by referring to the drama triangle (see Chapter 3). An SAEf (see Chapter 6) chart can again be a useful tool in planning how to intervene.

## VERBAL COMMUNICATION

Young people may need to learn the skills of relating to people, to conduct satisfying relationships by applying recognizable verbal and non-verbal skills. They may have missed the chance of learning productive language skills in day-to-day dialogue with adults, and they may have been cared for in the important early years by adults who themselves may have had restricted language opportunities. Children learn by example and we are their role models. We need to encourage and enable them to understand that there are other ways of relating.

### Emotional climate

Communication can be seriously hampered by a lack of awareness to the emotional climate. Our emotional state influences our perceptions of what is being said to us, and can block the process of communication. If we are wrapped up in our own feelings we will not be sensitive to the needs and feelings of others. We need to be responsive to the feelings of those we work with: colleagues as well as young people. In listening to young people we must make sure we hear their voices and respond with an open mind, not one that is closed by unquestioned assumptions.

### Developmental level

Language is a very powerful vehicle for reinforcing people's low self-esteem, for example, consider the use of critical and insensitive language by people in positions of power. We need to be attuned to the developmental level of the child. This relates to:

- different levels of understanding between adults and children
- differences amongst children according to their level of maturity
- differences amongst children in terms of intelligence, educational attainment and life experience.

There are no simple formulae to follow in judging the appropriate developmental level, so we need to become sensitive to these differences, which can undermine attempts to develop rapport and can alienate the child. Examples of how we do this are: speaking at a level above their heads (thereby undermining confidence and self-esteem) and patronizing them through speaking down to them.

## Vocal qualities

A considerable amount of information is conveyed not through what is said, but how we say it. The rate of speech, pitch, loudness and timbre of the person's voice speaks volumes. Try saying 'Go Away' or 'Shut Up' in as many different ways as possible and it is easy to recognize that often it is not so much what is said that matters, but how it is said.

## Non-verbal communication

It has been suggested by some language experts that up to 85 per cent of communication is non-verbal, through tone of voice and inflection, body language, etc. It is helpful to reflect on the language that we use and the way we use that language.

## Skilled communication

Skilled communication is essential. It is easy to take communication for granted, after all we spend a great deal of every day talking to and communicating with others. However, when faced with challenging behaviour, there is no doubt that how and what we communicate makes a huge difference. Many situations become less troublesome, because adults employ a range of communication skills in the face of disturbing, perhaps dangerous behaviour. Two skills are briefly considered here.

### Reflective communication

Use of reflective communication provides an opportunity to use feeling words and increases emotional literacy. Listen carefully for the feelings that the child is expressing, be tentative, reflect those feelings back to the child. Reflective communication can be as simple as saying, 'I think you feel… (*state the feeling word*)'.

### Assertive communication

The child's challenging behaviour can make us feel like reacting in extreme ways. We may feel angry and punitive and respond in authoritarian ways, trying to use coercive discipline and punishment to switch off the unwanted behaviour, or we may feel overwhelmed and powerless, unsure about how to respond in case we make matters worse. Of course, what we need to be able to do is to be authoritative, that is, to clearly explain what the child is doing, how it impacts on us, and what alternatives we would prefer, without withdrawing respect by showing the child that they are less valued as a person because of their behaviour at this time. This can be expressed in a form of words such as: 'When you…(*non-judgemental statement of child's behaviour*) I feel…(*honest description of feelings*). I would like you to…(*alternative*)'.

This could be something like this: 'When you are angry and you spit at me, I feel dirty. I would like you to tell me how angry you are without trying to hurt me'. Using planned forms of words may seems false and cumbersome, but having a rehearsed script can help us slow down emotionally and not be reactive to the threat posed by the child's challenging behaviour. By practising a script we begin to become so familiar with it that it sounds natural. We also begin to use other ways of saying the same thing that are more in our own words.

By naming your feelings in response to the challenging behaviour, you present an assertive response to the child that is emotionally honest. It allows the child to become aware of the effect their disturbing behaviour is having on others, to be challenged in their actions, but avoids increasing confrontation by giving commands, by criticising or by asserting adult power. This form of words also enables the child to identify their own inner experience by learning to communicate feelings and needs, and to recognize that others also have feelings and needs.

## PARENTING SKILLS

So far this chapter has looked at the relationships, dynamics and schemas underlying challenging behaviour. This understanding shapes the beliefs and assumptions, and the ways of caring that contribute to the child's developmental niche. But caring and informed adults also need a set of practice skills with which to deliver these underlying ideas. Parenting skills that promote consistent and predictable responses promote secure base experiences that facilitate recovery and earned security within the child. By dealing effectively and safely with challenging behaviour we help the child to acquire a feeling of earned security within the relationship. We turn our attention now to a set of parenting skills that can be acquired and used when working to manage challenging behaviour.

## Validation

Validation involves affirmation, confirmation and recognition of the child's experiences, communicating that you recognize and understand how the child is feeling and are not trying to persuade them to feel differently. It is important to validate the child's feelings at the same time as being clear that unacceptable behaviour is unacceptable: 'It is OK to be angry, but it is not OK to hurt someone/break things because we feel angry'.

## Praise

Try to catch the child doing good things (we usually manage to catch them when they're doing bad things!) Always show appreciation of co-operation and provide direct incentives (such as some of your time) for good behaviour. Avoid generalized praise ('You've been good this week'). Be specific, naming what they've done well ('You put your shoes in the cupboard when I asked', 'When you got angry you didn't hurt anybody/break anything'). Don't forget that the child can get as much of your time and attention as they need by kicking off. It is the thing they most want. Give them as much as you can when they are doing well. However, do no undermine the currency of praise through over-use.

## Positive messages

Reward good behaviour when you can; focus more on what the child has done well, and less on what they have done badly. A reward is not a bribe. If we offer the child a reward for not doing something, we are going to encourage them in that behaviour in order to earn rewards for stopping. This is a bribe. It encourages controlling and punitive behaviour, and can harden the behavioural organization, which is attempting to resolve the sense of fear without solution that pervades disorganized attachment. However, a reward is given to a child for achieving something that is difficult for them. The best rewards are small; praise, recognition and encouragement are often enough. Avoid endless tangible rewards, which feed an over-materialistic view of the world and encourage a hollow narcissism that suggests to the child that only material objects, not warm relationships, are of value. When the child is challenging, respond to the person and as far as possible ignore the challenging behaviour. Acknowledge compliance, and as far as possible, ignore non-compliance.

## Following the rule

When we tell a child not to do something, we assume they know what it is you wish them to do instead. If they do not, they are left bewildered and are unlikely to comply, as they feel unable to read our mind. Instead, help the child find a way out by telling them what you want them to do, not what you don't, and how they are to do it. 'We walk in the house' is better than, ' Don't run!'. ' If you come down from the fence we can play over here ' is better than 'Get down from there!'. 'Sit with the chair legs on the floor' is better than 'Don't swing on the chair!'

## Two good choices

Structure choices for the child by giving two good choices; for example, 'When you've done 'A' (*less attractive choice, like making the bed*) you can do 'B' (*more attractive choice, like play in the garden*)'. Avoid any form of threat or consequence, for example, 'If you don't do 'A', you can't do 'B'.

## Giving choice

Locate responsibility with the child; 'I need you to make the bed. We can't go out until you do'.

## Visual supports

Although visual supports should be introduced gradually, presenting information to individuals in a visual way can encourage and support communication and the development of language. It can also help to promote independence, build confidence and raise self-esteem. Visual supports need to be appropriate to the individual and in line with their needs and current stage of development. You can use sequences or schedules to break down activities into component parts, to take a child step by step through a particular procedure, for example, and you can use them for much more extended activities. Visual supports are very personal and what works for one may not work for another. If you find a preferred type of visual representation (e.g. photos, drawings, symbols, real objects) it is more accessible and less confusing to use it consistently in all environments. Visual support can be provided through hand gestures and facial expressions, for example, thumbs up and smile, thumbs down and frown. We can also use photographs, drawings, coloured pictures, written words, toys, miniatures and real objects.

## Prioritizing

Don't endlessly pick up a child for their behaviour. Ask your self, 'Does this behaviour need to be dealt with?' Decide on the important behaviours to challenge.

# GOLDEN NUGGETS FOR MANAGING CHALLENGING BEHAVIOUR

These are in no particular order:

- Listen.
- Always keep in mind how the child is feeling.
- Maintain a low-arousal environment.
- Be consistent, predictable, nurturing, stimulating and set and maintain explicit boundaries.
- Value and listen to children, respect their rights, but be clear about the distinction between children and adults based on recognition of learning and development achieved.
- Leave a way out, with dignity and choice.
- Contain your own anxiety, keep yourself calm.
- Respond to the person, ignore the challenging behaviour.
- Acknowledge compliance, ignore the challenge.
- When things are getting out of control, control the things that you can, don't worry about the things you can't, although you may need to act to keep safe.
- Decide whose problem it is.
- Work out consistent attitudes and responses ahead of problems.
- Don't enter into battles you can't win.

- Don't see disagreements as always being a battleground.

- Don't use sweeping generalizations.

- Be specific about behaviours that are a problem and separate them from the person. Unacceptable behaviours are just that, unacceptable, but the child also needs unconditional positive regard.

- Remember who is the adult.

- Try to catch your child behaving well and reward them with praise and attention.

- Make praise specific: say what they've done well rather than just a general 'You're doing well'.

- Children model their behaviour on adults, so observe how we behave.

- Have an ethical, honest, respectful, valuing attitude as if it is reciprocal and mutual, but don't expect anything back just now.

- The worse the level of behaviour, the smaller the sanctions.

- Use small repeatable sanctions.

- Don't make threats 'You do this, I will (or won't) do that'.

- Don't say you will do things you can't/won't/think differently about later.

- Describe feelings.

- Communicate empathetically.

- Have fun when you can.

## Chapter Eight

# Changing Problem Behaviour

Child-centred and effective interventions can be developed to encourage change and facilitate recovery. The emphasis is on communication with the child and their active involvement in the change process and developing strategies that can be successfully employed to encourage change in problem behaviours.

## LEARNING OUTCOMES FOR THIS CHAPTER

Once you have studied this chapter you should be able to:

- ensure warmth and support are intrinsic to modifying unwanted behaviours
- develop effective, non-punitive discipline
- ensure that children and adults feel valued, and that children are involved in change
- develop the use of therapeutic approaches to managing and changing behaviours
- use time-in to modify behaviour and problem-solve
- develop effective reward programmes to modify behaviour and promote secure base experiences and organized mental representation.

## APPROACHES TO CHANGING PROBLEM BEHAVIOUR

In residential and foster care, and in schools for children with emotional and social difficulties, approaches to changing problem behaviour rooted in social learning theory are widespread. These approaches reward wanted positive behaviours through privileges and reward, and remove privileges or apply sanctions for unwanted negative behaviour.

This approach may be effective if children have some internal controls, and are willing and able to adapt to a set of pro-social rules. However, lacking inner control or a coherent, organized representation of caregivers as safe and trustworthy, children with highly anxious and disorganized attachment mistrust authority figures and view such approaches as untrustworthy. They lack motivation to change to achieve rewards, and respond with apathy, combativeness, isolation and depression to a system that primarily emphasizes control.

However, control is not unimportant. Without some external control the child cannot feel safe, and therefore cannot explore their relationships, past and present. Control therefore needs to focus on ways that promote safety, are individually responsive to the child, and foster an organized mental representation of caregivers as a safe haven: responsive, warm, empathic and valuing.

Authoritative parenting defines the adult–child relationship as an alliance to the child's benefit and is seen in assertive responses to problem behaviour. Many problem behaviours can be seen as rooted in unmet attachment needs, often resulting from poor inhibition and a lack of impulse control. They may work well enough for the child in that they serve the function of exerting control over, or punishing, adults, and can reflect the behavioural organization post-infancy that is characteristic of disorganized attachment.

Adults charged with caring for the troubled child are likely to identify a great many problem behaviours. Thoughts and feelings that are difficult to express may be acted out. The child will not change their problem behaviours just because we want them to. Endlessly corrected, the child will believe that they are endlessly in the wrong, and can do nothing right. Their identity and their coping mechanisms will be under attack, and they are likely to collapse or retaliate. Some poorly attached children will seek out attention however negative it is. Confrontation and spiralling conflict are assured ways of getting a great deal of attention. The child may be addicted to the hormonal rush that accompanies strong, unregulated emotions.

Sometimes it is better to accept modifying unwanted behaviours than to expect to remove them completely. Our expectations should be realistic; focusing on a few big behaviours that matter is more effective than trying to change them all.

We are not infallible, and may be drawn into conflict and a battle of wills with the children we are looking after. Be clear what the child does, who they affect, who this is a problem for, and why. Avoid any sense of the child being somehow wrong; it is their behaviour that is the issue. Gaining the child's collaboration to tackle behaviours that present a problem for them or for others means that changes are more likely to be durable and to apply across settings and environments.

## STRATEGIES, TECHNIQUES AND APPROACHES

Caregivers' predictable and consistent responses to unwanted behaviour promotes organized mental representation within the child of the caregiver as a safe haven, and encourages exploration in the knowledge that the caregiver will intervene when the child needs them to manage and control their behaviour. Good therapeutic work needs skilled behaviour management in order to balance proximity as a response to danger, and exploration as a response to safety and growing autonomy. Over time, these experiences develop self-worth and earned security within the child. Therapeutic work should not be mystified. Much of what is required is good parenting, but always backed up with a reflective approach from caregivers and thoughtful understanding of the child's attachment difficulties and their often chaotic inner world. In order to work with each individual child's complex difficulties, caregivers need a range of approaches.

### Planned ignoring

Planned ignoring is often misunderstood and dangerously misapplied; if the child feels they are being ignored they have a huge range of behaviours to re-engage you. Most of these behaviours are an escalation of the problem. If they started by swearing and end up breaking windows because we've ignored them, whose problem is that? Children who have unresolved feelings of loss and separation are likely to experience us ignoring them as us abandoning them. Somehow we need to ignore the behaviour but not the child, remaining sensitively responsive to the child's unmet needs.

However, planned ignoring can be very effective. It is the unwanted behaviour that is ignored, not the child. There are five aspects to consider when using planned ignoring:

1. Take absolutely no notice of behaviours such as rude remarks and protests.

2. Ignore tantrums, shouts and screams by wherever possible leaving the child alone. Tell the child where you're going to be and under what conditions you will return. Be specific and avoid exerting power (e.g. 'I'm not leaving you alone, I'm just going to sit next door, I'm going to come back when you've stopped shouting'). The idea is to let them gain control of themselves once their behaviour is no longer being rewarded by our interaction.

3. Give them occasional reassuring messages, without commenting on the behaviour. ('I'm looking forward to spending some time with you, but I need you to stop kicking the doors first' – withdraw once again.)

4. Time limit if possible. The child needs to experience some way back to reattunement. Their internal working model predicts that this will not happen. Surprising them by forgiving them (reattunement) allows for the experience of reintegrative shame.

5. Try to get on with your own affairs. This can often best be some simple homely task like tidying (vacuum cleaners can be very useful). If the child attempts to join in, let them if they are not being aggressive or disruptive. They may be trying to establish reattunement. If they try to disrupt your task, try acting as if they are helping, it sometimes works, but avoid sarcasm (e.g. you start vacuuming, the child unplugs the vacuum cleaner, you say, 'That's OK, I want to plug this in over there now').

## Time-out

Time-out is sometimes considered as a cause/effect therapeutic technique to isolate the child when their behaviour is unacceptable or out of control, which provides an opportunity for the worker to create distance between them and the child. Time-out is, technically, time out from reinforcers of undesirable behaviour. So, any removal of the child from the reinforcers by moving the child, or any removal of the reinforcers from the child's space, would have as its goal the extinction of the behaviour produced by those reinforcers. However, a time-out might reinforce earlier experiences in which the child has felt unwanted and abandoned, while the caregiver's removal signifies that they do not have sufficient empathy for the child's situation, intensifying previous feelings of rejection. In place of time-out what the child needs is time-in. This can take two forms: 'time-limited removal' and 'time-in with the engaged self'. The first uses breaking attunement to exert discipline, the second provides the opportunity to establish attunement to provide support.

## Time-limited removal

Time-limited removal works well for relatively low-level difficult behaviours that are great enough to need to be dealt with, but not so problematic that a longer intervention is required. It provides removal from the reinforcers without reinforcing earlier experiences of being abandoned. It should be strictly time limited (three minutes is often about right). The child is removed from the stimuli but the adult remains with them, or in close proximity to them, signalling that the child is still held in mind and that the caregiver is keeping them close to protect from threats. Remain sensitive to their mood, ignoring the problem behaviour but not the child. The child learns that safety can be predictably found in the caregiver, and security can develop.

The adult breaks attunement, as a consequence of their behaviour, but provides reattunement once the child has experienced this for a short, time-limited period. The child has an opportunity to experience reintegrative shame. The time limit begins once the child is removed from the stimulus and the adult has shown that they are no longer attuned to the child (e.g. by sitting calmly and quietly, in an emotionally neutral manner) not when the child is complying. In this way we easily gain some control over the situation, as it is about our actions, not the child's. If we wait for the child to comply, they may take a very long time, leaving their problem behaviour in control of us.

Once the time is up, acknowledge that the child has been removed from the stimulus for as long as you've asked and tell them what is next. What is next needs to provide the opportunity for reattunement, as this is the process that the infant experiences as reintegrative shame ('That's good, you've come away from the others for three minutes, now we can go back to the garden to play').

The skill is not to be too easily re-engaged by the child (as if their behaviour doesn't have any consequences) but not to be coldly rejecting, hostile or punitive, and to control the moment when you allow reattunement. A short time period is best; you can always repeat the process. If the child tries to engage us during the time-in period, we should employ attentive silence, which might include a head nod, a calming hand gesture, a therapeutic grunt and a simple statement of, 'Three minutes', backed up by scripts such as, 'I'm just going to sit here quietly with you for a few moments. I'm happy to talk about what's just happened, if you want, but I don't really want to just talk pleasantly to you until you've sat out for three minutes'. Attentive silence can be repeated several times. The child experiences that the time-in will end when we said, that they are not forgotten about, but they cannot control or punish us. For example:

> Adult: (*head nod, calming hand gesture*) 'um-um, three minutes.'
>
> Child: 'You***! I'm going to***!'
>
> Adult: 'Three minutes.'
>
> Child: 'I want to go and play!'
>
> Adult: (*head nod, calming hand gesture*) 'um-um, three minutes.'
>
> Child: '** that!'
>
> Adult: 'I'm going to sit here quietly with you for a few moments. I'm happy to talk about what's just happened, if you want, but I want you to wait for three minutes before we do.'

## Time-in with the engaged self

The second form of time-in with the caregivers, 'time-in with the engaged self' allows us to work out our differences with the child, and is not time limited. It begins with a message such as, 'This isn't going very well for either of us, why don't we go to (*name the place*) and see what we can do to get things back on track for you'. Depending on circumstances workers may like to take the child outside to a quiet part of the garden, or out on a walk or for a drive. The child is more likely to explore the problem with you if they know in advance that they have a safe haven to visit and a steam valve for strong feelings that emerge. Side-by-side (rather than face-to-face) rhythmic activities are particularly useful for this: walking, a short trip in the car, sitting on swings. The worker can remain sensitive to the child's body language and voice tone without the child feeling that a hostile and judgemental adult is watching them.

The balance is to provide a safe setting that provides the opportunity for the child to do something soothing (lowering their state of arousal and yours) without providing a treat. We should be clear that spending time with children who are having difficulties is not rewarding their problem behaviour with our time, it is a strong message that we will stick with them, not abandon them, and that we want to, and can, help them.

It is all right for us to admit that we are momentarily unsure how to proceed (if we are); at this point it is more important than ever that the child and the worker work together to get through the differences at hand. The major issue is not to shun the child; rather it is to acknowledge that there's a need for a close time, in which both can begin to learn skills for potential understanding and possible compromise. Time-in begins to achieve this end.

## BEHAVIOUR MODIFICATION CHARTS

It is important to acknowledge that behaviour that is modified by rewards or sanctions may well reappear in a different environment as the feelings and thoughts that underlie the behaviour may not have changed. Having said that, behaviour modification charts can be effective, not least because they can allow the child to break out of an endless negative cycle of failure and criticism. Used well, behaviour modification charts can be a practical expression of our holding the child in mind, signal our proximity in symbolic ways, and contribute to a sense of predictability and consistency, which promotes safety and secure base experiences, as well as providing challenge and exploration.

### Star charts

A star chart is a simple, visual chart that allows a child to see their progress towards pre-agreed goals and rewards. Stars, or some other symbol, are added each time the child achieves a goal. Usually, the stars can add up over a period towards some small, tangible reward. Star charts (or similar) work for two basic reasons, because children love them, and because they provide a positive way (using encouragement and praise) to tackle issues, breaking the cycle of nagging and telling off that it is so easy to fall into as parents, carers and educators.

Generally it is better to reward the behaviour you want to see, rather than sanction the behaviour you don't. Concentrate on one or two, or a maximum of three, behaviours you want to encourage. Be clear, both to yourselves and to the child, what these behaviours are. Explain why they are good behaviours to develop. Think in terms of the child's developmental level and have achievable expectations so that you can build on the child's success, but don't set expectations so low that there is no challenge to their current level of behaviour. Have short time scales, both for the number of days and for the parts of days. If the programme is not effecting measurable change in a short time, review it. Be prepared to alter it, or discontinue it; endlessly not getting a reward for not achieving targets does not motivate change.

It is important that failure early in the chart does not remove incentives for later success, but don't change the goals or allow earn backs. In the face of the child's distress or anger at not achieving their target, caregivers can become entangled, and fearing the pain of the child's rejection, find them a way of earning back some of their missed reward. This does not help them. Safely contain their distress or anger does. Be sure you have time to make a considered decision before you decide. Never decide on the score when you are angry or upset. It's better to say, 'I'm not sure, I want to have some time to calm down and think about it', than make a rash decision.

Reward all achievements of expectations. Find rewards that are real incentives. It can be helpful if the child picks from a menu of equivalent rewards. For younger children, lots of small rewards work best, but older children may be able to wait for longer (but find out, don't assume this). Don't forget that the chart itself is a reward; your time, involvement and praise count for an awful lot. Such charts also provide easily understood, visual feedback to the child about what they are achieving. It is essential that they are accurate and honest.

Involve the child in the design of the chart. Its visual appeal is important. Valuing their input shows that you value the child and emphasizes that it is their behaviour, their chart and their reward.

Star charts can be effective in tackling a range of everyday issues. They do not have to involve stars and can work with most age groups. Star charts can help establish desired behaviours such as: a good bedtime routine, regular teeth cleaning, completion of homework, educational achievements: reading, writing, telling the time, learning times tables, etc. They can also be used to reduce problem behaviour such as: hitting, telling tales, thumb sucking, and refusing to help with household chores.

## Star charts golden rules

- Find a format that is age appropriate. Even adolescents can benefit from the idea, but the challenge is to present it in a way that is not patronizing.

- Stick to one issue and be realistic. Only tackle one issue at a time and always make sure that the goal you are setting for the child is realistic and achievable within a three to four week timeframe.

- Make expectations low enough in the beginning for the child to succeed. Then, slowly raise the expectations. If the standards are too high, the child will get frustrated and the effort will fail.

- Think about ways you can help the child succeed.

- Involve the child before you start using a chart – they must want to tackle the issue and must also understand how the chart is going to work.

- Stay positive and concentrate on praising success.

- Rewards should be simple and inexpensive. They can be daily or based on accumulation of charts during the week for a specified reward on a specified day. Be creative. Examples are stickers, snacks, free time, staying up late for a story, or verbal praise.

- Never take away stickers or rewards, and be consistent in the way rewards are given.

- If you are worried about any issue always ask for help or advice.

Make sure that you understand exactly what behaviour you are focusing on, and be realistic about what the child can achieve in the short term. It's important to define the problem in clear, practical terms. For example, we want the child to 'behave at mealtimes' or 'be nice to their peers'. This could be expressed as a list of things to do:

- Wash our hands before we sit down at the table.

- Ask someone to pass the things we want.

- Pass things when asked.

- Stay sitting at the table until everyone has finished.

Children have to enjoy the system to make it work, and that can only happen if the expectations allow them to be successful. It is important to think through why the child will want to use the chart. Simply telling them why you think it's a great idea won't work. There are four basic things that will motivate a child and these need thinking about in advance, and discussing with the child:

- The fun of owning and using a chart. The chart needs to be a fun design and fun activity. Your attention is an important part of this too.

- Achieving the goal that benefits the child like waking up dry, or having more friends.

- Being praised; most children love to be praised and to please other people. Some children who are insecurely attached and traumatized do not.

- Getting a reward. This can be as simple as collecting the stars, but it is a very good idea to offer some form of rewards for success too. Importantly, this should be something the child wants; but it should be a little treat rather than a huge present.

It is also important that you now help the child as much as possible with the issue you're trying to tackle. It's a good idea to do some background research into what may help them succeed; there are almost certainly things you can do to boost their chances of success. Done well, star charts focus on:

- effective, two-way communication

- promoting pride of accomplishment

- earning respect and benefits

- accepting, and learning from, consequences.

### Star charts: a word of caution

Not all children are motivated by star charts. They may not work for children who are highly traumatized, or with a highly anxious or disorganized attachment, as these children do not generally have the internal controls or motivation to succeed that such charts require. Misapplied, a star chart presents further evidence to reinforce their IWM as ineffective. Some children who are compulsively compliant will initially say that they want to take part in such a behaviour modification, but will tend to become enraged, either over the progress of the chart, or some other seemingly unrelated matter, as a way of deflecting from their inner wish not to comply.

A star chart should never be enforced; it is a collaborative exercise to change a behaviour the child wishes to change as well. If you begin, and are having adverse reactions, you need a way out. Calmly acknowledge to the child that you don't think it is working, and ask for their perspective. If they say it is, you will need to pin them down to what they think they are achieving and how you can further help them. If they feel it isn't working, empathize with how difficult it is to change long embedded-behaviours, and explain that you will try to help them find other ways of making progress that don't require charts. Reassure the child that they are valued for themselves, and that the star chart was about changing behaviour, not about judging them.

## Traffic lights

Traffic lights differ from star charts. The name comes from a rudimentary diagram and the symbolic use of red, amber and green (see Figure 8.1). In most cases, children will help design other images: perhaps sun and

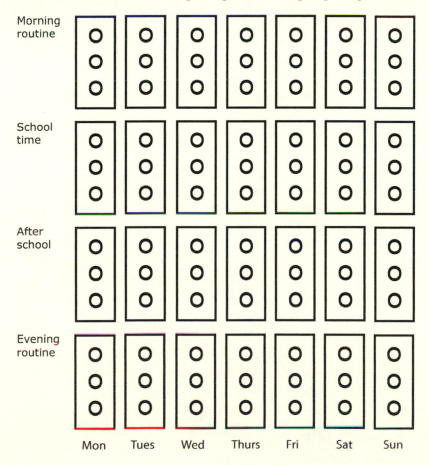

Figure 8.1: Traffic lights

clouds, ships with varying loads, cars and varying passengers. Many designs will do. Involve the child, and use your imagination. Whichever is chosen, it needs to be able to show three levels of achievement at each point on the chart and relate to the timeframes that you are using.

Although traffic lights incorporate rewards, they are longer-term interventions than star charts. They are for communicating a child's behaviour (for the child and the adult) and to promote reflection, rather than being a behavioural reward system. They do not rely on the child's (lacking) inner controls, nor do they require the child's motivation in the same way as star charts. Over time they tend to promote motivation within the child and reward developing self-control, and provide predictability and consistency. They promote self-worth and allow adults to be real and truthful about a child's functioning and interactions without becoming negative or punitive.

Traffic lights provide the opportunity to give rewards for good behaviour and to sanction unwanted behaviour, but sanctions should never be given as a result of the scores on the chart. The sanction (or consequence) is the score. The child has the opportunity to learn that behaviour has consequences (good and bad) and adults have a safe way of showing their disapproval of certain behaviours. This provides a useful stream-valve for adults and child. The adults can release any feelings of frustration and disempowerment, and the child can express their frustration at the adult's external controls over small enough matters not to induce large-scale conflict.

Traffic lights deal with expectations, provide opportunity for clear explanation, and allow unconditional expression of warmth, and so reinforce the model of authoritative parenting. As with other behaviour charts, they need to avoid becoming global dumping grounds and be focused specifically. It is important that the child understands the system, and although they work well from ages six to 18, they need to be individually adapted to be effective. They can be applied to meeting specific expectations, and are highly effective if linked to an Individual Support and Development Plan (ISDP) as outlined in Chapter 3.

Typically, the day would be divided into four sessions and the chart would cover a week. Younger children may need more sessions in a day, and may need a daily, not weekly chart. The traffic lights allow three scores:

- met expectations linked to reward system (green)

- met expectations with support (amber)
- did not meet expectations (red).

This allows the child not to feel they have failed completely over small things. They are being encouraged to try and meet expectations and accept support. They are not being rewarded for complying, or achieving easily. This enables recognition of the child beginning to internalize self-control (amber), and provides an effective sanction (a red) that does not feed their sense of pervasive shame.

It is essential that adults are consistent in the way that scores are applied. This requires some discussion and perhaps some leadership. The consistent and predictable response that is embedded in well-used traffic lights allows the child to organize their understanding of how their actions make others feel. This encourages mind-mindedness and helps the child organize their attachment experiences. It is essential that the middle condition 'met expectations with support' is fully understood. This can be illustrated by referring to the final line of the excerpt in Chapter 3 (see Figure 3.2). Ben is expected to behave in a sociable way during meals. If he does so he earns a green mark, if he does not he earns a red. So what is 'met with support'? The caregivers' role is to provide support and guidance to each child in the group. If Ben responds to this support and guidance through the meal, he receives amber. He needs some chance to try, depending on his emotional maturity, but not endless chances so that the adult rescues him. The effect of his functioning on his score does not need to be mentioned at the time (this may not be support, but an attempt to coerce). What works is very individual, and carers will often know their child well enough to have good interventions. Ben may need messages that remind him of the expectation and explanation and project sufficient warmth, such as 'Ben, I can see you're unsettled, I know you can sit and eat a meal with the rest of us, perhaps you need to take a deep breath and calm down'.

As well as providing a system for rewards, the chart monitors the child's behaviour and allows them to see, in a visual format, how they have met expectations over the week. Regular feedback to the child on the information on the chart is essential. This requires honesty and empathy, for example: 'It's been a difficult week, I can see you've had some reds. Do you remember what you were doing here (*ask about a red*)? Do you remember what you were feeling? Could we have helped you in any way at that time? But you've got some greens, that's very good, and these yellows show that you were really making an effort...' The process provides a calm sense of order and allows an unconditional response to the child not meeting expectations. This promotes an organized internal mental presentation of caregivers as safe havens, promoting exploration, and providing support when required.

A simple way to calculate a reward is to give a numeric value to green (3), amber (2) and red (0). This weights the score towards meeting expectations with support, which represents progress for the child. On the chart above, this is a maximum score of 84. By relating this to what you expect the child to score currently, you can have two or three levels of rewards (perhaps 74–84, 64–74, 54–64). Rewards should be small; much of the advice on rewards and star charts applies.

Don't discount the reward inherent in achieving within this system, or the reinforcing effect of praise and encouragement. If the system includes tangible rewards it is important to stress that these should be small items, not huge gifts, that the child should have some voice in the reward (perhaps by picking from a menu, or some children enjoy a lucky-dip box) and that the score that earns a reward should be achievable. You can use an incremental approach to this, perhaps starting at no more than 50 per cent reds and decreasing that percentage over time as the child succeeds. You can have a reward for one score and a bonus for exceeding it by a pre-agreed amount.

You can use your and the child's imagination, but make sure that everything is agreed before the chart starts. As this system can run over prolonged periods, it is important that you review and change it as the child makes progress, always keeping it focused on what the priority is for the child at the time. But do not make unplanned or spontaneous changes. Ensure that the child is involved in the changes, underlining that once they have achieved one target they can move on to another. Emphasize how this system has helped them understand their behaviour and change in a good way. You don't have to stick to traffic lights.

# Bibliography

Addison Stone, C. (1993) 'What is Missing in the Metaphor of Scaffolding?' In D. Faulkner, K. Littleton and M. Woodhead (eds) (1998) *Cultural Worlds of Early Childhood.* London and New York: Routledge.

Adshead, G. (2001) 'Murmurs of Discontent: Treatment and Treatability of Personality Disorders.' In G. Adshead and C. Jacob (eds) (2009) *Personality Disorder: The Definitive Reader.* London and Philadelphia: Jessica Kingsley Publishing.

Agrawal, H.R., Gunderson, J., Holmes, B.M. and Lyons-Ruth, K. (2004) 'Attachment studies with borderline patients: a review.' *Harvard Review of Psychiatry 12,* 2, 94–102.

Ainsworth, M. (1985) 'Patterns of infant-mother attachments: antecedents and effects on development.' *Bulletin of New York Academy of Medicine 61,* 9, 771–90.

Ainsworth, M. (1993) 'Attachment as related to mother–infant interaction.' *Advances in Infancy Research 8,* 1–50.

Ainsworth, M. and Bell, S. (1970) 'Attachment, exploration and separation: illustrated by the behaviour of one-year-olds in a strange situation.' *Child Development 41,* 1, 49–67.

Ainsworth, M., Blehar, M., Water, E. and Wall, S. (1978) *Patterns of Attachment: A Psychological Study of the Strange Situation.* Oxford: Lawrence Erlbaum.

Ainsworth, M. and Bowlby J. (1991) 'An ethological approach to personality development.' *American Psychologist 46,* 4, 333–341.

Alderman, T. (1997) *The Scarred Soul: Understanding and Ending Self-inflicted Violence.* New York: New Harbinger Publications.

American Psychiatric Association Staff (2000) *Diagnostic and Statistical Manual of Mental Disorders, DSM-IV-TR (4th edn, text revision).* Arlington: American Psychiatric Publishing Inc.

Aristotle (Translated by J.R. Ackrill, J.O. Urmson and Sir D. Ross) (1998) *The Nicomachean Ethics.* Oxford: Oxford World's Classics.

Atkinson, R.L., Atkinson, R.C., Smith, E.E., Bern, D.J. and Nolen-Hoeksema, S. (1999) *Hilgard's Introduction to Psychology (13th edition)* London: Harcourt College Publishing.

Axline, V. (1971) *Dibs. In Search of Self.* London: Penguin.

Azmitia, M. (1997) *Interactive Minds: Life-span Perspectives on the Social Foundation of Cognition.* Cambridge: Cambridge University Press.

Barnes, P. (1995) *Personal, Social and Emotional Development of Children.* Oxford: Blackwell.

Bates, J. E. (1989) 'Concepts and Measures of Temperament.' In G.A Kohnstamm, J.E. Bates and M.K. Rothbart (eds) *Temperament in Childhood.* Wiley: Chichester.

Bell, R.Q. (1968) 'A reinterpretation of the direction of effects in studies of socialization.' *Psychology Review* 75, 81–95.

Belsky, J. and Steinberg, L. (1978) In P. Barnes (1995) 'The effects of day care: a critical review.' *Child Development 49,* 929–949.

Berne, E. (1964) *Games People Play: The Basic Handbook of Transactional Analysis.* New York: Random House.

Berne, E. (1997) (Nineteenth edition) *What Do You Say After You Say Hello.* Corgi: London.

Bernier, A. and Meins, E. (2008) 'A threshold approach to understanding the origins of attachment disorganization.' *Developmental Psychology 44,* 4, 969–982.

Betleheim, B. (1974) *A Home for the Heart.* London and New York: Thames and Hudson.

Bettelheim, B. (1950) *Love is not Enough.* New York: The Free Press.

Biddulph, S. (1997) *Raising Boys.* London: Thorsons.

Bion, W. (1962) *Learning from Experience.* London: Heinemann.

Blake, R. and Mouton, J. (1964) *The Managerial Grid: The Key to Leadership Excellence.* Houston: Gulf Publishing Co.

Blurton Jones, N. (ed.) (1972) *Ethological Studies of Child Behaviour.* London: Cambridge University Press.

Bowlby, J. (1965) (Second edition) *Child Care and the Growth of Love.* London: Pelican.

Bowlby, J. (1988) *A Secure Base: Clinical Applications of Attachment Theory.* Abingdon: Routledge.

Bowlby, J. (1989) *The Making and Breaking of Affectional Bonds.* London: Tavistock Publishing.

Bowlby, J. (1997) *Attachment and Loss (Vol. 1 Attachment).* London: Random House Pimlico. (Original work published 1969.)

Bowlby, J. (1998a) *Attachment and Loss (Vol. 2 Separation: Anger and Anxiety).* London: Random House Pimlico. (Original work published 1973.)

Bowlby, J. (1998b) *Attachment and Loss (Vol. 3 Loss, Sadness and Depression).* London: Random House Pimlico. (Original work published 1980.)

Bradley, C. (2001) 'Making Sense of Symbolic Communication.' In A. Hardwick and J. Woodhead (eds.) (2001) *Loving, Hating and Survival: A Handbook for All who Work with Troubled Children and Young People.* Aldershot: Ashgate.

Bradshaw, J. (1972) *The Concept of Social Need. New Society 496,* 640–643.

Brown, R. (1986) (Second edition) *Social Psychology.* London: The Free Press.

Burton, J. (1990) *Conflict: Human Needs Theory.* London: Macmillan.

Cairns, K. (2002) *Attachment, Trauma and Resilience: Therapeutic Caring for Children.* London: BAAF.

Camras, L. A.A., Grow, J. G. and Ribordy, S.C. (1983) 'Recognition of emotional expression by abused children.' *Journal of Clinical and Child Psychology 12*, 3, 325–8.

Carlson, E. (1998) 'A prospective longitudinal study of attachment disorganization/disorientation.' *Child Development 75*, 66–83.

Carlson, E.A. (1998) 'A prospective longitudinal study of disorganized-disoriented attachment.' *Child Development 69*, 4, 1107–1128.

Carter, R. (2000) *Mapping the Mind.* London: Phoenix.

Chibucos, T. and Kail, P. (1981) 'Longitudinal examination of father–infant interaction and infant–father interaction.' *Merr-Palmer Quarterly 27*, 81–96.

Clements, J. and Zarkowska, E. (2000) *Behavioural Concerns and Autistic Spectrum Disorders, Explanations and Strategies for Change.* London: Jessica Kingsley Publishers.

Clough, R., Bullock, R. and Ward, A. (2006) *What Works in Residential Child Care.* London: NCERCC and National Children's Bureau.

Colby, A., Kolberg, L., Gibbs, J. and Lieberman, M. (1983) 'A longitudinal study of moral judgement.' *Monographs of the Society for Research in Child Development 48*, 1–2, Serial No 200.

Cole, M. (1992) 'Culture in Development.' In M. Woodhead, D. Faulkner and K. Littleton, (eds) (1998) *Cultural Worlds of Early Childhood.* London and New York: Routledge.

Crick, N.R., Murray-Close, D. and Woods, K. (2005) 'Borderline personality in childhood: a short-term longitudinal study.' *Development and Psychopathology 17*, 1051–1070.

Crittenden, P.M. (2005) 'Attachment theory, psychopathology, and psychotherapy: the dynamic-maturational approach.' *Teoria dell'attaccamento, psicopatologia e psicoterapia 30*, 171–182.

Crittenden, P.M. (2006) 'A dynamic-maturational model of attachment.' *Australia and New Zealand Journal of Family Therapy 7*, 2, 105–115.

Crokenbourg, S. and Litman, C. (1990) 'Autonomy as competence in two-year olds: maternal correlation of child defiance, compliance and self-assertion.' *Developmental Psychology 26*, 961–971.

Cunningham, P. and Page, T. (2001) 'A case study of a maltreated thirteen-year-old boy: using attachment theory to inform treatment in a residential program.' *Child and Adolescent Social Work Journal 18*, 5.

Darwin, C. (1998) *On the Origin of the Species: By Means of Natural Selection.* Hertfordshire: Wordsworth Classics. (Original work published 1859.)

Das Gupta, P. 'Images of Childhood and Theories of Development.' In J. Oates (ed.) (1994) *The Foundations of Child Development.* Oxford: Blackwell/Open University.

Davies, M. and Wallbridge, D. (1990) *Boundary and Space: An Introduction to the Work of D.W. Winnicot.* London: Karnac.

De Haas, M.A., Bakermans-Kranebourg, M.J. and van Ijzendoorn, M.H. (1994) 'The Adult Attachment Interview and questionnaires for attachment style, temperament, and memories of parental behavior.' *Journal of Genetic Psychology 155*, 4.

Department of Health (2007) *Best Practice in Managing Risk: Principles and Evidence for Best Practice in the Assessment and Management of Risk to Self and Others in Mental Health Services.* National Risk Management Programme.

De Zulueta, F. (1999) 'Borderline personality disorder as seen from an attachment perspective: a review.' *Criminal Behaviour and Mental Health 9*, 237–253.

Delfos, M.D. (2004) *Children and Behavioural Problems.* London: Jessica Kingsley Publishers.

Dockar-Drysdale, B. (1990) *The Provision of Primary Experience.* London: Free Association Books.

Dodge, K.A. (1986) 'Social Information-processing and Assessment of Social Competence in Children.' In C. Zahn-Waxler, E.M. Cummings and R. Ianotti (eds) *Altruism and Aggression.* Cambridge: Cambridge University Press.

Donaldson, M. (1978) *Children's Minds.* London: Fontana.

Dunn, J. (1991) 'Young Children's Understanding of Other People: Evidence from Observations Within the Family.' In M. Woodhead, D. Faulkner and K.Littleton (eds) (1998) *Cultural Worlds of Early Childhood.* London and New York: Routledge.

Erikson, E. H. (1950) *Childhood and Society.* New York: Norton.

Erikson, E.H. (1968) *Identity Youth and Crisis.* London: Faber and Faber.

Fahlberg, V.I. (1991) *A Child's Journey Through Placement.* Indianapolis: Perspectives Press.

Faupel, A. Herrick, E. and Sharp, P. (1998) *Anger Management, A Practical Guide.* London: David Fulton.

Felce, D. and McBrien, J. (1991) *Challenging behaviour and Severe Learning difficulties.* First Draft Publications, Kidderminster: BILD

Feshbach, N. D. (1987) 'Parental Empathy and Child Adjustment/Maladjustment.' In N. Eisenberg and J. Strayer (eds) *Empathy and its Development.* Cambridge: Cambridge University Press.

Fonagy, P., Gergely, G. and Target, M. (2007) 'The parent–infant dyad and the construction of the subjective self.' *Journal of Child Psychology, Psychiatry and Allied Disciplines 48,* 3–4, 288–328.

Fonagy, P., Leigh, T., Steele, M., Steele, H., Kennedy, R., Mattoon, G., Target, M. and Gerber, A. (1996) 'The relation of attachment status, psychiatric classification and response to psychotherapy.' *Journal of Consulting and Clinical Psychology 64,* 1, 22–31.

Fonagy, P., Target, M., Gergely, G., Allen, T.G. and Bateman, A.W. (2003) 'The developmental roots of borderline personality disorder in early attachment relationships: a theory and some evidence.' *Psychoanalytic Enquiry 23,* 3, 412–459.

Forehand, R. and McMahon, R. J. (1981) *Helping the Non-compliant Child.* New York: Guildford Press.

Fraley, C. and Shaver, P.R. (2000) 'Adult romantic attachment: theoretical developments, emerging controversies, and unanswered questions.' *Review of General Psychology 4,* 2, 132–154, 1089–2680. *Educational Publishing Foundation 2000.*

Fraley, R.C. (2002) 'Attachment stability from infancy to adulthood: meta-analysis and dynamic modelling of developmental mechanisms.' *Personality and Social Psychological Review 6,* 2, 123–151.

Fruzzetti, A.E., Shenk, C. and Hoffman, P.D. (2005) 'Family interaction and the development of borderline personality disorder: a transactional model.' *Development and Psychopathology 17,* 4, 1007–30.

Gagne, R.M. and Berliner, D.C. (1988) (Fourth edition) *Educational Psychology.* New Jersey: Houghton Mifflin.

Gauvin, M. (1995) 'Thinking in Niches: Sociocultural Influences on Cognitive Development.' In D. Faulkner, K. Littleton and M. Woodhead (eds) (1998) *Learning Relationships in the Classroom.* London and New York: Routledge.

George, C., Kaplan, N. & Main, M. (1984), Adult Attachment Interview Protocol. Unpublished manuscript, University of California, Berkeley. Cited in Prior, V. & Glaser,

D. (2006). *Understanding Attachment and Attachment Disorders: theory, evidence and practice.* London: Jessica Kingsley

George, C., Kaplan, N. & Main, M. (1985). Adult Attachment Interview Protocol (Second edition) . Unpublished manuscript, University of California, Berkeley. Cited in Prior, V. & Glaser, D. (2006). *Understanding Attachment and Attachment Disorders: theory, evidence and practice.* London: Jessica Kingsley.

George, C., Kaplan, N. & Main, M. (1996). Adult Attachment Interview Protocol (Third edition). Unpublished manuscript, University of California, Berkeley. Cited in Prior, V. & Glaser, D. (2006). *Understanding Attachment and Attachment Disorders: theory, evidence and practice.* London: Jessica Kingsley.

George, C. and Soloman, J. (1996) 'Representational models of relationships: links between caregiving and attachment.' *Infant Mental Health Journal 17,* 3, 198–216.

Gershoff, E.T. (2002) 'Corporal punishment by parents and associated child behaviors and experiences: a meta-analytic and theoretical review' *Psychological Bulletin, The American Psychological Association 128,* 4, 539–579.

Gillath, O., Selcuk, E. and Shaver, P. R. (2008) 'Moving toward a secure attachment style: can repeated security priming help?' *Social and Personality Psychology Compass 2/4,* 1651–1666.

Goffman, E. (1959) *The Presentation of Self in Everyday Life.* New York City: Anchor Books.

Goffman, E. (1961) *Asylums: Essays on the Social Situation of Mental Patients and Other Inmates.* New York City: Anchor Books.

Golding, K.S., Dent, H.R., Nissim, R. and Stott, L. (2006) *Thinking Psychologically About Children Who Are Looked After and Adopted – Space for Reflection.* Hoboken: John Wiley and Sons.

Goleman, N. D. (1996) *Emotional Intelligence: Why It Can Matter More Than IQ.* London: Bloomsbury.

Grant, A., Mills, J., Mulhern, R. and Short, N. (2004) *Cognitive Behavioural Therapy in Mental Health Care.* Los Angeles: Sage.

Green, R. G. (1990) *Human Aggression.* Milton Keynes: Open University Press.

Gross, R. (2004) (Third edition) *Psychology: The Science of Mind and Behaviour.* London: Hodder and Stoughton.

Gubman, N. (2004) 'Disorganized attachment: a compass for navigating the confusing behaviour of the "difficult-to-treat" patient.' *Clinical Social Work Journal 32,* 2, 159–169.

Harter, S. (1987) 'The determinants and mediational role of global self-worth in children.' In N. Eisenberg (ed.) (1983) *Contemporary Topics in Developmental Psychology.* New York: Wiley.

Heim, A. (1970) *Intelligence and Personality: Their Assessment and Relationship.* Harmondsworth: Penguin.

Henderson, J. and Atkinson, D. (eds) (2003) *Managing Care in Context.* London: Routledge.

Herbert, C. and Wetmore, A. (1999) *Overcoming Traumatic Stress.* London: Constable and Robinson Ltd.

Herbert, M. (1991) *Clinical Child Psychology.* Chichester: Wiley.

Herman, J. L., Perry, J. C. and van der Kolk, B. A. (1989) 'Childhood trauma in borderline personality disorder.' *American Journal of Psychiatry 146,* 490–495.

Hesse, E. (1996) 'Discourse, memory and the Adult Attachment Interview: a note with emphasis on the emerging cannot classify category.' *Infant Mental Health Journal 17*, 4–11.

Hinde, R.A. (1989) 'Temperament as an Intervening Variable.' In G.A. Kohnstamm, J.E. Bates and M.K. Rothbart (eds) *Temperament in Childhood.* Chichester: Wiley.

Hoffman, M. L. (1987) 'The Contribution of Empathy to Justice and Moral Judgement.' In N. Eisenberg and J. Strayer (eds) *Empathy and its Development.* Cambridge: Cambridge University Press.

Holmes, J. (2003) 'Borderline personality disorder and the search for meaning: an attachment perspective.' *Australia and New Zealand Journal of Psychiatry 37,* 524–531.

Holmes, J. (2004) 'Disorganized attachment and borderline personality disorder: a clinical perspective.' *Attachment and Human Development 6,* 2, 181–190.

Holowenko, H. (1999) *Attention Deficit/Hyperactivity Disorder.* London: Jessica Kingsley Publishers.

Hopson, B. and Adams, J. (1976) 'Towards an Understanding of Transitions.' In J. Adam and B. Hopson (eds) *Transition: Understanding and Managing Personal Change.* London: Martin Robertson.

Howe, D. (2003) *Child Abuse and Neglect: Attachment Development and Intervention.* New York: Palgrave Macmillan.

Hughes, D.A. (1997) *Facilitating Developmental Attachment.* New Jersey: Jason Aronson.

Hughes, D.A. (2007) *Attachment-Focused Family Therapy.* New York and London: W.W. Norton and Co.

Izzard, C.E. (1971) *The Face of Emotion.* New York: Appleton-Century-Croft.

Jellema, A. (2000) 'Insecure attachment states: their relationship to borderline and narcissistic personality disorders and treatment process in cognitive analytic therapy.' *Clinical Psychology and Psychotherapy 7,* 138–154.

Jewett Jarratt, C. (1982) *Helping Children Cope with Separation and Loss.* Harvard Common Press: Boston.

Johnson, B. (2005) *Emotional Heath.* Ventnor: Trust Consent Publishing.

Johnson, B. (2006) *Unsafe at Any Dose.* Ventnor: Trust Consent Publishing.

Kahan, B. (1994) *Growing Up in Groups.* London: HMSO.

Kennerley, H. (2000) *Overcoming Childhood Trauma.* London: Constable and Robinson Ltd.

Kirkland, J., Bimler, D. and Klohnen, E. (2005) Paper presented at Fourteenth Biennial Australasian Human Development Conference, Perth.

Kitwood, T. (1997) *Dementia Reconsidered. The Person Comes First.* Open University Press: Buckingham.

Kohlberg, L. (1969) 'Stage and Sequence: The Cognitive-developmental Approach to Socialization.' In D.A. Goslin (ed) *Handbook of Socialization Theory and Research.* Chicago: Rand-McNally.

Kuczynski, L. (1984) 'Socialization goals and mother–child interaction: strategies for long-term and short-term compliance. *Developmental Psychology 20,* 1061–1073.

Levy, K. N. (2005) 'The implications of attachment theory and research for understanding borderline personality disorder.' *Development and Psychopathology 17,* 939–986.

Liotti, G. (2004) 'Trauma, dissociation, and disorganized attachment: three strands of a single braid.' *Psychotherapy: Theory, Research, Practice Training 41,* 4, 472–486.

Long, N.J. (1995) 'Why adults strike back: Learned behavior or genetic code?' *Reclaiming Children and Youth 4*, 1, 11–15.

Lorenz, C. (1966) *On Aggression*. London: Methuen.

Lyons-Ruth, K. (2008) 'Contributions of the mother–infant relationship to dissociative, borderline and conduct symptoms in young adulthood.' *Infant Mental Health Journal 29*, 3, 203–218.

Lyons-Ruth, K., Melnick, S., Patrick, M. and Hobson, R.P. (2007) 'A controlled study of Hostile-Helpless states of mind among borderline and dysthymic women.' *Attachment and Human Development 9*, 1, 1–16.

Lyons-Ruth, K. and Spielman, E. (2004) 'Disorganized infant attachment strategies and helpless-fearful profiles of parenting: integrating attachment research with clinical intervention.' *Infant Mental Health Journal 25*, 4, 318–335.

Lytton, H. and Zwirner, W. (1975) 'Compliance and its controlling stimuli observed in a natural setting.' *Developmental Psychology 11*, 769–779.

McCartney, K., Tresch Owen, M., Booth, C., Clarke-Stewart, A. and Lowe Vandell, D. (2004) 'Testing a maternal attachment model of behaviour problems in early childhood.' *Journal of Child Psychology and Psychiatry 45*, 4, 765–778.

Maier, H. W. (1979) 'The core of care.' *Child Care Quarterly 8*, 3, 161–173.

Main, M. and Cassidy J. (1988) 'Categories of response to reunion with the parent at age six: predictable from infant attachment classifications and stable over a one-month period.' *Developmental Psychology 24*, 3, 415–426.

Main, M. and Solomon, J. (1986) 'Discovery of an insecure-disorganized/disoriented attachment pattern.' In T.B. Brazelton and M.W. Yogman (eds) *Affective Development in Infancy*. Norwood: N.J. Ablex.

Makela, J. (2003) 'What makes theraplay effective: insights from developmental sciences.' *Theraplay Institute Newsletter*. Fall/Winter.

Malatesta, C.Z. and Haviland, J. M. (1982) 'Learning display rules: the socialization of emotional expression in the first two years of life.' *Monographs of the Society for Research in Child Development 50*, 1–2.

Marcia, J.E. (1980) 'Identity in Adolescence.' In J. Adeleson (ed.) *Handbook of Adolescent Psychology*. New York: John Wiley.

Marris, P. (revised edition 1986) *Loss and Change*. London: Routledge and Kegan Paul.

Maslow, A. (1970) *Motivation and Personality*. New York: Harper and Row.

Maslow A (1987) (Third edition) *Motivation and Personality*. New York: Harper and Row.

Maslow, A. (1988) *Toward a Psychology of Being*. Hoboken: John Wiley and Sons.

Mayhew, J. (1997) *Psychological Change*. Basingstoke: Macmillan.

Miller, A. (1987) *For Your Own Good: The Roots of Violence in Child Rearing*. London: Virago.

Miller, E. J. (1993) 'Creating a Holding Environment: Conditions for Psychological Security.' Cited in A. Ward and L. McMahon (eds) (1998) *Intuition is not Enough*. London: Routledge.

Norton, K. (1996) 'Management of Difficult Personality Disordered Patients.' In G. Adshead and C. Jacob (eds) (2009) *Personality Disorder: The Definitive Reader*. London and Philadelphia: Jessica Kingsley Publishers.

Oates, J. (1994) 'First Relationships.' In J. Oates (ed.) *The Foundations Of Development*. Oxford: Blackwell/The Open University.

Ogawa, J.R., Sroufe, L.A., Weifield, N.S., Carlson, E.A. and Egeland, B. (1997) 'Development and the fragmented self: longitudinal study of dissociative symptomatology in a non-clinical sample.' *Development and Psychopathology 9,* 4, 855–879.

Parke, R. D. and Tinsley, B.J. (1981) 'The Father's Role in Infancy: Determinants of Involvement in Caregiving and Play.' In M.E. Lamb (ed.) (Second edition) *The Role of the Father in Child Development..* New York: Wiley.

Parkes, C.M. (1986) *Bereavement: Studies of Grief in Adult Life.* London: Tavistock Publishing.

Parkes, C.M., Stevenson-Hinde, J. and Marris, P. (1991) *Attachment Across Life Cycle.* London: Routledge.

Patrick, M., Hobson, R.P., Castle, D., Howard, R. and Maughan, B. (1994) 'Personality-disorder and the mental representation of early social experience.' *Development and Psychopathology 6,* 2, 375–388.

Patterson, G. R. and Forgatch, M. (1987) *Parents and Adolescents: Living Together.* Toronto: Castilia Press.

Pavlov, I. P. (1928) *Lectures on Conditioned Reflexes, Vol. I.* London: Lawrence and Wishart.

Piaget, J. and Inhelder, B. (1969) *The Psychology of the Child.* London: Routledge and Kegan Paul.

Piaget, J. (1970) *Biology and Knowledge.* Edinburgh: Edinburgh University Press.

Prior, V. and Glaser, D. (2006) *Understanding Attachment and Attachment Disorders: Theory, Evidence and Practice.* London: Jessica Kingsley Publishers.

Reich, D.B. and Zanarini, M.C. (2001) 'Developmental aspects of borderline personality disorder.' *Harvard Review of Psychiatry 9,* 6, 294–301.

Rest, J.R. (1983) 'Morality.' In P.H. Mussen (ed.) *Handbook Of Child Psychology. 3: Cognitive Development.* New York: Wiley.

Rocissano, L., Slade, A. and Lynch, V. (1987) 'Dyadic synchrony and toddler compliance.' *Developmental Psychology 23,* 698–704.

Rogers, C. R. (1955) *Client Centred Therapy.* New York: Houghton Mifflinn.

Rogers, C. R. (1967) *On Becoming a Person: a Therapist's View of Psychotherapy.* London: Constable.

Rogers, C. R. (1980) *Freedom To Learn For The 80s.* New York: Free Press.

Rogosch, F.A. and Cicchetti, D. (2005) 'Child maltreatment, attention networks and potential precursors to borderline personality disorder.' *Development and Psychopathology 17,* 1071–1089.

Rutgers, M., Bakerman-Kranenburg, M., van Ijzendororn, M. and van berkelaer-Onnes (2004) 'Autism and attachment: a meta-analytics review.' *Journal of Child Psychology and Psychiatry 45,* 1123–1134.

Sabini, J. (1995) *Social Psychology.* London: Norton.

Sameroff, A.J, and Chandler, M. J. (1975) 'Reproductive Risk and the Continuum of Caretaking Casuality.' In F.D. Harrowitz, Scarr-Salaptek, S. and Siegel, G. (eds) *Review of Child Development Research, 4.* Chicago: University of Chicago Press.

Schaffer, H.R. (1977) *Mothering.* London: Fontana.

Schaffer, H.R. (1996) *Social Development.* Oxford: Blackwell.

Schon, D. A. (1983) *The Reflective Practitioner: How Professionals Think in Action.* London: Temple Smith.

Sears, R.R., Rau, L. and Alpert, R. (1957) *Identification and Child-rearing.* Stanford, CA: Stanford University Press.

Seifer, R. and Schiller, M. (1996) Attachment, maternal sensitivity, and infant temperament during the first year of life.' *Developmental Psychology 32,* 1, 12–25.

Seiler, L. (2008) *Cool Connections with Cognitive Behavioural Therapy.* London: Jessica Kingsley Publishers.

Shaver, P. R., Belsky, J., and Brennan, K. A. (2000) 'Comparing measures of adult attachment: an examination of interview and self-report methods.' *Personal Relationships 7,* 25–43.

Skinner, B. F. (1973) *Beyond Freedom and Dignity.* Harmondsworth: Penguin.

Snarey, J. R. (1985) 'Cross-cultural universality of social-moral development: a critical review of Kohlbergian research.' *Psychological Bulletin 97,* 202–232.

Solomon, J., George. C. and De Jong. A. (1995) 'Children classified as controlling at age six: evidence of disorganized representational strategies and aggression at home and at school.' *Development and Psychopathology 7,* 447–464.

Sroufe, L. A., Carlson, E. A., Levy, A. K. and Egeland, B. (1999) 'Implications of attachment theory for developmental psychopathology.' *Development and Psychopathology 11,* 1–13.

Sroufe, L.A. and Waters, E. (1997) 'Attachment as an organizational construct.' *Child Development 48,* 4, 1184–1199.

Srouffe, L.A. (1998) 'The Role of Infant Care-giver Attachment in Development.' In J. Belksky and T. Nezworksi (eds) *Clinical Implications of Attachment.* New Jersey: Lawrence Erlbaum.

Stevens, A. (1998) *An Intelligent Person's Guide to Psychotherapy.* London: Duckworth and Co.

Stewart, R.B. (1983) 'Sibling attachment relationships; child–infant interactions in the strange situation.' *Developmental Psychology 19,* 192–9.

Super, C.M. and Harkness, S. (1982) 'The development of affect in infancy and early childhood.' In M. Woodhead, D. Faulkner and K. Littleton (eds) (1998) *Cultural Worlds of Early Childhood.* London and New York: Routledge.

Sutton, J. (2007) (Third edition) *Healing the Hurt Within.* Oxford: How to Books.

Sylva, K. and Lunt, I. (1982) *Child Development, A First Course.* Oxford: Blackwell.

Takie, W. (2001) 'How do deaf infants attain first signs?' In V. Lewis, M. Kellet, C. Robinson, S. Fraser and S. Ding (eds) (2004) *The Reality of Research with Children and Young People.* London: Sage/Open University.

Tharp, R. and Gallimore, R. (1991) 'A Theory of Teaching as Assisted Performance.' In M. Woodhead, D. Faulkner and K. Littleton (eds) *Learning Relationships in the Classroom.* London and New York: Routledge.

Thomas, A. and Chess, S. (1977) *Temperament and Development.* New York: Bremner Mazel.

Thompson, R.A. and Raikes, H.A. (2003) 'Toward the next quarter-century: conceptual and methodological challenges for attachment theory.' *Development and Psychopathology 15,* 691–718.

Torgersen, S., Lygren, S., Øien, P.A., Skre, I., Onstad S., Edvardsen, J., Tambs, K. and Kringlen, E. (2000) 'A twin study of personality disorders.' *Comprehensive Psychiatry 41,* 6 416–425.

Trevarthern, C. (1995) 'The child's need to learn a culture.' In M. Woodhead, D. Faulkner and K. Littleton (eds) (1998) *Cultural Worlds of Early Childhood.* London and New York: Routledge.

van Ijzendoorn, M.H. and Bakermans-Kranenburg, M.J. (2003) 'Attachment disorders and disorganized attachment: similar and different.' *Attachment and Human Development 5*, 3, 313–320.

van Ijzendoorn, M.H., Schuengel, C. and Bakers-Kranenberg, M.J. (1999) 'Disorganized attachment in early childhood: meta-analysis of precursors, concomitants, and sequelae.' *Development and Psychopathology 11*, 225–246.

Vaughn, B., Egeland, B., Sroufe, L.A. and Waters, E. (1979) 'Individual differences in infant–mother attachment at 12 and 18 months: stability and change in families under stress.' *Child Development 50*, 971–975.

Vygotsky, L. S. (1962) *Thought and Language*. Cambridge Mass: M.I.T. Press.

Walker, L. J. (1989) 'A longitudinal study of moral reasoning: a critical review.' *Child Development 55*, 677–691.

Ward, A. (1993) *Working Together in Group Care*. Birmingham: Venture Press.

Ward, A. (1998) 'Helping Together.' In A. Ward and L. McMahon (eds) *Intuition Is Not Enough*. London: Routledge.

Ward, A. (2003) 'The Core Framework.' In A. Ward *et al. Therapeutic Communities for Children and Young People*. London: Jessica Kingsley Publishers.

Ward, A. and McMahon, L. (eds) (1998) *Intuition is not Enough*. London and New York: Routledge.

Waters, H.S. and Waters, E. (2006) 'The attachment working models concept: among other things, we build script-like representations of secure base experiences.' *Attachment and Human Development 8*, 3, 185–197.

Webb, D. and McMurran, M. (2008) 'Emotional intelligence, alexithymia and borderline personality disorder traits in young adults.' *Personality and Mental Health 2*, 265–273.

Webster-Stratton, C. (2003) *The Incredible Years*. Seattle: Incredible Years.

Weeks, D. (1992) *The Eight Essential Steps to Conflict Resolution*. New York: Putnam.

Weinfield, N. S., Whaley, G. J. L and Egeland, B. (2004) 'Continuity, discontinuity, and coherence in attachment from infancy to late adolescence: sequelae of organization and disorganization.' *Attachment and Human Development 6*, 1, 73–97.

Wellman, H.M. (1990) *The Child's Theory of Mind*. New York: Bradford Books/MIT Press.

Wesiner, T.S. and Gallimore, R. (1997) 'My brother's keeper: child and sibling caretaking.' *Current Anthropology 18*, 169–90.

Whiting, B. B. and Edwards, C.P. (1998) *Children of Different Worlds: The Formation of Social Behaviour*. Cambridge, MA: Harvard University Press.

Winnicott, D.W. (1956) 'The Anti-Social Tendency.' In *Through Paediatrics to Psychoanalysis: Collected Papers*. London: Karnac Books and the Institute of Psychoanalysis.

Winnicott, D. (1965) *The Maturational Process and the Facilitating Environment*. London: Hogarth Press.

Wolf, S. (1969) *Children Under Stress*. London: Penguin.

Wood, D. (1986) 'Aspects of Teaching and Learning.' In M. Richards and P. Light (eds) *Children of Social Worlds*. Cambridge: Polity Press.

Wood, D. (1988) *How Children Think and Learn*. Blackwell: London.

World Health Organisation (1993) *ICD-10 Classification of Mental and Behavioural Disorders: Diagnostic Criteria for Research*. Geneva: World Health Organisation Publishing.

Wright, H. (1989) *Groupwork: Perspectives and Practice*. London: Scutari Press.

Young, J. E., Klosko, J.S. and Weishaar, M. E. (2003) *Schema Therapy: A Practitioner's Guide.* New York and London: Guildford Press.

Youniss, J. (1994) 'Children's Friendships and Peer Culture.' In M. Woodhead, D. Faulkner and K. Littleton (eds) (1999) *Making Sense of Moral Development.* London and New York: Routledge.

Zilberstein, K. and Messer, E.A. (2007) 'Building a secure base: treatment of a child with disorganized attachment.' *Clinical Journal of Social Work.*

# Index